SUPERTANKER

SUPERTANKER

LIVING ON A MONSTER VLCC

DR RAY SOLLY

The History Press

Cover illustrations: **Front:** An overhead view of *Rania Chandris* (Fotoflite)
Back: A freshly painted *Rania Chandris* ready to set sail. (Odense
Steel Shipyard)

First published 2019

The History Press
97 St George's Place
Cheltenham, GL50 3QB
www.thehistorypress.co.uk

British Library Cataloguing in Publication Data.
A catalogue record for this book is available from the British Library.

ISBN 978 0 7509 8769 1

Typesetting and origination by The History Press
Printed and bound in Great Britain by TJ International Ltd.

CONTENTS

ACKNOWLEDGEMENTS

I never sailed with BP Tankers, but am greatly indebted to BP Plc photographic library at the University of Warwick for their unreserved help in providing archive photographs supporting my story. These images illustrate admirably the bridge watch-keeping, shipboard operations, and lifestyle germane to tankers of all classes, but they highlight specifically the range of some of these duties performed aboard VLCCs in the 1970s.

Gratitude and fond memories are retained of both Captain 'Tommy' Agnew, the superb ship's master of *Rania Chandris*, and Derek Allan, a chief officer of expertise, immeasurably calm patience and temperament. Serving under such officers eased my learning of a new trade.

PROLOGUE

Oil was first discovered in America in 1859 and within just three years the world's first cargo of crude oil was carried in barrels by sea between the Delaware River and London aboard the British sailing brig *Elizabeth Watts*. I joined Chandris of England's Very Large Crude Carrier (VLCC) *Rania Chandris* in the summer of 1973, but undoubtedly the political changes witnessed during the intervening period of little more than 100 years out of our world's history were breathtaking. The greatest result was an almost instantaneous demand for a fuel that was cleaner, cheaper and more efficient than coal. Whilst initially the uptake occurred in America and Europe, it soon became international.

Almost immediately the sailing brig proved totally inadequate for the job. This led over the next fifty or so years to the evolution of a new brand of ship called 'the tanker', but equally as quickly, problems emerged that were complex and initially difficult to solve. It was soon discovered that crude oil emitted hydrocarbon gases that were both highly explosive and toxic, which made it extremely dangerous to carry by ship. But working out ways to overcome this difficulty was not the only task confronting those involved in finding solutions arising from the new method of conveyance. Transatlantic sea passages of around fifty days were involved and it became essential to transport the cargo in sufficient quantities to make the trip economically viable.

This became even more important as markets expanded. Although oil was being discovered in other areas of the world, a further difficulty arose from where it appeared on the earth's surface. These places were not only inhospitable but far removed from the refineries where it was required. Although ingenious American thinking had led early on to the construction of a pipeline, it would be many years before this method of transporting oil caught on more widely internationally. In the meantime, the only option was to rely on the ship.

Numerous experimental 'new-fangled vessels' (as a shipping magazine of the day unkindly described the craft) soon evolved and these underwent as many constructional changes as the human embryo. But in 1910, the English marine architect Sir Joseph Isherwood, a Lloyd's surveyor for twelve years, devised a hull form that proved a major breakthrough. His tanker departed from the standard-built vessels to date by improving the length to depth relationship of the ship's hull. Basically, Isherwood introduced a system of longitudinal bulkheads divided by transversals that resulted in a number of oil-tight tanks consistent with the length of the tanker. Isherwood's designs, which he modified in the 1920s, gave the industry a stronger vessel with transversal web frames in each tank and enhanced corner brackets. It was in the 1920s also that a second longitudinal bulkhead was introduced, and the combined package produced the now conventional layout of a number of integrated sets of one centre and two wing tanks that served as a model for the standard tanker virtually without modification for the next seventy years.

By the late 1930s, a 'standard' tanker had evolved that was constructed on Isherwood's design, resulting in a ship of around 12,000 deadweight tons capacity with an average length of 486ft. In 1942, demands for tankers to replace appalling losses of ships during the Second World War led to an original Esso Tanker Company design being resurrected by American yards that gave a new, quickly built and comparatively cheap tanker called the 'T2' class. More than 500 of these mass-produced tankers, with a capacity of around 18,600 tons and length of 439ft on a reduced draught, were propelled by steam turbine engines and served international markets. Although constructed initially with just one Atlantic crossing planned, many were still familiar sights in the world's shipping lanes fifty years later.

From the 1950s, demands for oil exploded. The gradual transition from coal as the main source of international energy created monumental changes in private, industrial and commercial demand, which had to be reflected in an increase in the size and capacity of tankers. New building techniques fired by the American Daniel Ludwig working through Japanese shipbuilding yards saw the world's first 100,000-ton tanker launched in 1959. Just seven years later, the first 200,000-ton tanker also appeared from Japanese yards, followed in 1968 by the world's first 326,585-ton tanker in the shape of Ludwig's *Universe Ireland*.

It was around 1973 that London tanker freight brokers, working through their Average Freight Rate Assessment (AFRA) panel acting for the chartering of tankers, divided the various sizes of tankers into categories by tonnage. They were the first to give to the world's shipping markets the term Very Large Crude Carrier, or VLCC for short, covering those tankers between 160,000 and 300,000 tons. The British-flagged *Globtik London* and *Globtik Japan*, each exceeding 476,000 tons, also appeared on the scene in that year.

This bumper year saw the launch of a ship that would bring the industry into the public domain and help turn supertankers and a specific ship into a household name. The ship was the *Jahre Viking*, to use the most famous of a number of name changes ascribed to this monster. She was built by the Oppama Shipyard in Japan and was launched, after a few ownership problems, in 1975 at 418,610 tons with a length of 376.73m. In 1973 the Shell and Esso tanker companies launched what AFRA would designate the following year as Ultra Large Crude Carriers, or ULCCs, as category for ships exceeding 300,000 tons. This modest fleet of monsters owned by the two oil companies, each exceeded 500,000 tons, but it was not until 1980 that the *Jahre Viking* was lengthened to 485.85m, giving her a deadweight tonnage on her summer draught marks of 564,763 tons. She was the largest moving object devised by man and the shipping press all too soon ran out of superfluous descriptions in their efforts to outdo each other when they referred to her.

By the time I had joined *Rania Chandris* in the summer of 1973, oil had become an essential commodity with ever increasing worldwide demand: it would be no exaggeration to say that human civilisation then – and now – would simply grind to a halt without it.

CHAPTER ONE

MEETING THE MONSTER

My initial sighting of the VLCC *Rania Chandris* as the local aircraft from Copenhagen to Elsinore in Denmark came into land revealed what seemed to be an island attached to a large concrete jetty. Looking down on the recently completed supertanker offered a gull's eye view. Actually seeing this vessel close up really focused my mind. I could not believe the size of it, she was colossal! I had been told by fellow mariners these vessels were the largest moving objects devised by man, but after serving as a navigating officer aboard dry-cargo ships of 7,000–10,000 gross registered tons (grt) and averaging 450ft overall length, I simply could not visualise taking this 145,000grt, 1,139.2ft long (or 347.2m, virtually a quarter of a mile) monster to sea – and being responsible for her safe navigation.

The theory of voyage planning did not bother me over-much for this would be close to the requirements normal for any vessel, apart from paying *much* closer attention to depths of water below the hull. Anyway, I had already made easily enough in my seafaring life a fairly difficult professional and social transition from navigating deep-sea ships to the profoundly unique idiosyncrasies then associated with coastal trading, so I did not envisage too many problems going in the other capacity direction, as it were. No, my thoughts were fired by the reality of actually seeing this sheer bulk of ship. The sight refocused concerns regarding

what might confront me when entering the wheelhouse door and taking responsibility for two sea-going navigational watches totalling eight hours a day. I pondered specifically how this giant might handle under way when altering course. I tried to think positively, for at least my previous concerns of absorbing brand new cargo procedures and coping with standby operations on a massive forecastle or after-deck were forced into insignificance. I recall suddenly having 'butterflies in the stomach' that were completing somersaults while I was wondering just what the hell I had let myself in for. Suddenly, those smaller dry-cargo ships and a familiar way of life seemed almost friendly!

Left and opposite: Although under way in these shots, the views correspond directly to the initial sighting of Rania Chandris *as the local aircraft from Copenhagen flew over the ship as it came into land at Elsinore. (Fotoflite)*

I was to discover these would not be the only shocks I experienced during the course of my following years' service aboard this class of ship. I remain unsure to this day what prescience might have motivated me into keeping comprehensive records of nearly everything that happened professionally on board during my first three tours with *Rania Chandris*. Certainly, that first glimpse could not foresee how my records could indicate an international gestation period that would turn these vessels from evolutionary large crude oil carriers into revolutionary ships. Nor how concerns merely hinted at in those days regarding environmental pollution and drunken crews would lead to a gradual monitoring of social behaviour and introduce computerised systems, complex safety devices, and stringent regulations that would alter drastically the construction from single to double-hull ships, operational practices and cargo handling/engineering techniques on the world's fleet of VLCCs. Nor could I begin even to forecast how such essential interventions might turn the oil-tanker industry into the most highly regulated form of transportation in the world. And how, in turn, this would pave the way for unexpected offshoots affecting safety aboard the products and chemical tanker fleets: dry-cargo carriers, container ships and passenger liners to affect even the laissez-faire attitude towards seafaring practices I had experienced aboard coastal vessels.

So, giving the radio officer a dry lopsided grin expressing a relaxed humour that frankly was not felt, but nevertheless outwardly sharing his clear excitement, I retook my seat and reflected on the circumstances leading to this present situation.

My adventure had begun innocently enough while on leave between voyages. During coffee one morning, while glancing through that bastion of maritime information, the journal *Lloyd's List*, my idle eyes were captured by an insignificant advertisement in the situations vacant column:

Navigating and Engineering officers required immediately for very large crude oil carrier. Tanker experience preferred.

Apply to Box xxxx Lloyd's List and Shipping Gazette.

I had always wanted to navigate VLCC-class vessels, colloquially known as supertankers, but my companies to date had served only deep-sea dry-cargo trades. Often casting almost lustful eyes, I had passed close by these monsters or had seen them on distant horizons and had chatted with officers serving aboard them by Aldis lamp or more recently VHF, so this advert jumped from the page to hit me foursquare between the eyes. A few printed words, it seemed, could possibly offer my chance. Undeterred by the 'tanker experience' aspect (or lack of it) but prepared for disappointment, my application was in the post next day.

Just two days' later, a phone call invited me for interview the following day 'if, of course, you are available' with Captain Ivan Branch, the marine superintendent serving Chandris Tankers of England, at 5 St Helen's Place, Bishopsgate in London. It seemed the shipping company based in Piraeus, Athens, were owners of a number of cruise liners (for which they remain renowned), plus a second fleet of assorted 7,000–8,000grt dry-cargo and product tankers. This London–Greek concern was expanding its existing collection of VLCCs and had purchased the latest addition from an ambitious Maersk Line that seemingly had over-ordered. At 286,000 summer deadweight tons (sdwt), *Rania Chandris* was to be the company's largest vessel, hence flagship of the fleet, and would carry its senior master as commodore. Having just been launched, she was lying in the fitting out berth at Odense Steel Shipyard, Elsinore, some 20 miles north of Copenhagen, Denmark, awaiting completion.

The super paused before examining my qualifications, discharge book and record of sea service to date and asked bluntly, in 'a seamanlike manner': 'Why have you applied for a position for which you are not even remotely qualified?'

I answered quite simply: 'I always wanted to serve aboard tankers and applied to Caltex among a few dry-cargo companies, but one of the latter was first to offer a deck cadetship so this was accepted. I remain enthusiastic about tankers and believe the fundamentals could soon be learnt.'

Taking this on the chin, he gave me a penetratingly direct look and mentioned it might be helpful to me (and the ship!) if I would consider joining as an extra officer for one voyage until I could be trusted with my fair share of cargo watches.

'Your saving grace,' Captain Branch continued, 'lies in the amount of time still outstanding for the tanker to complete her fitting out, and anyway – should we both agree to your joining – then being on board over this period would offer excellent opportunities for you to learn general tanker routines and become acquainted with the structure of the ship prior to working with Danish officers and ratings during sea trials.'

It became apparent that afterwards I would join the other officers attending the handing over ceremony – and share its delicious cele-bratory dinner. Then, even before ink had dried on the certificates and with the Danish flag changed for the Red Ensign, she would sail for the Arabian Gulf and my subsequent tour of her maiden and second voyages.

As our interview progressed he elaborated on the manning scales. Chandris was comparatively unique as a VLCC owner because the company deck-officered ships of this class with a master and four per-manent navigators. This was unlike many contemporary oil majors, who usually retained voyage traditions of three deck officers, often putting on an extra man for the run after Las Palmas when tank cleaning took place. They would then, if the tanks were completed ready for preload-ing inspection, fly him home either from Cape Town or an appropriate Arabian Gulf port.

Captain Branch's brows furrowed while clearly coming to a further decision. Looking directly at me (once again), he advised, 'Basically, if you are prepared to join the ship on third officer's salary and doing his job then, after a first tour of two voyages totalling about four months, you would go on two months' leave hopefully to be promoted upon your return for further tours.'

I rather liked the way he assumed we were already professionally wedded – it seemed to imply (and inspire) an inordinate measure of confidence with me and in me! He concluded that were I happy with his offer then I could sign a contract and in a few days the company would fly me out to Odense.

Distant sightings of numerous VLCCs while on passage aboard dry-cargo ships had whetted my appetite to serve on ships of this class. (Fotoflite)

My agreement and signing of the already prepared papers took only a few seconds. As I was in London where this new building was registered at Lloyd's Shipping Registry, and on the Shipping (Officers) Federation pool in nearby Mansell Street, a quick call could be made for clearances, including a medical. Phoning my dry-cargo employers next day, they were far from happy with my unexpected decision to part company with them: in fact, they were livid. However, having cast my die, five days' later I was at Heathrow, having arranged to meet our radio officer to board a BEA jet taking us to Copenhagen for an onward local flight to join the ship. It seemed Sparks and I, along with the other officers, would be berthed in local lodgings for a few days until our accommodation on board was habitable.

★ ★ ★

Ben, our Sparks, was an experienced radio officer employed by Marconi Marine, who supplied the radio equipment for the vessel. He was about 50 years of age, and married with teenaged children. This would be his first experience of tanker life and I found myself warming to his cheerfully relaxed temperament.

Our arrival at the lodging house was fortuitous, for we just had time to go into our comfortably adequate rooms and unpack before the remainder of the officers arrived from the ship for supper at the end of a lengthy days' work. Meeting new colleagues over the deck officers' table was little different from the norm with which I had been accustomed since joining that transient existence constituting the Merchant Navy. My immediate contacts socially had to be these other mates with whom I would work directly, taking friendships with the engineers, Sparks and the chief hunk (or steward) as these occurred. So we initially appraised each other quite warily, for there always resided a doubt regarding personalities, and how these might or might not intermingle over what could prove a potentially lengthy trip. But, as the meal developed with neutral experiences exchanged larded with adventures of past ships and voyages amidst numerous humorous anecdotes, so came the inevitable thaw. By the time we had finished coffee in the lounge each of us had agreed privately that the other was 'probably going to be worth living with'.

Derek, the chief officer, my immediate working boss, was a few years older than me, happily married with a young family and living in Devon. Similarly to the master, chief and second engineers, he had served his career to date aboard tankers and had also been recruited following an advert in *Lloyd's*. Having joined the ship nine weeks' previously, his inducement to sign on had been a promise of promotion to his own command of a later VLCC. I took to his quiet, warmly pleasing disposition immediately and felt inspired by his accepting confidence, so looked forward to learning and being guided by his vast tanker experience. Paul Tenbury, the second officer, was another tanker man. Recently married, he had been promised that on subsequent voyages he could bring along his wife, with the company generously footing the bill for her travel costs. We awaited the first officer, whom we understood was called Tim Wheeler, an ex-Mobil chief officer, who would be joining in a few days' time. Surrounded by all of this professional experience, I felt very much the 'new boy', although reassured that my colleagues would offer their help until I settled into new routines.

I stayed ashore that first night exchanging further reminiscences with the master of the vessel, Captain 'Tommy' Agnew. I had noticed over the meal table he had kept a wise silence, but was aware of his shrewd eyes taking in the interactions between his deck officers. Such casual chatting with him over a glass or two of Danish lager soon put my mind to rest. His open uncomplicated smile, direct eye contact and air of measured friendliness immediately drew my personality towards him. I had captured what seemed to be an amused glance flickering across his features as he listened to our conversations and guessed he had detected instinctively something of my uncertainty and appreciated the cause. Quite soon into our casual chatting he asked me directly if I had seen the ship from

Captain Agnew, an ex-commodore master from Esso Tankers, was the finest among many highly professional captains under whose command I served. (J. Shou)

the aircraft and, taking my affirmative on board, gently pointed out: 'You will find, Mr Solly, the sea soon cuts her down to size once away from land, even during your first solo bridge watch. Then, once deep sea, you will see that she will handle much like any other vessel, but you'll have to think ahead more than on a smaller ship before altering course. It would help your confidence were you to take her off automatic pilot now and then, put her on manual and "feel" the handling of the vessel in ballast and under different loaded conditions.'

He did not have to add 'Don't worry' – for I was not! The master confirmed Chandris Tankers was 'a good firm to work for', particularly with its manning arrangements of an extra deck officer because this freed the mate for permanent day work, of which he assured me (with that warm grin I would come to recognise only too well) 'there was a-plenty, and not only for Derek but also all of you mates!' He told me the company followed normal maritime practices for navigating officers, so I would be responsible for the eight-to-twelve watches, having taken over from the first officer and being relieved subsequently by the second.

Captain Agnew's perspicacity was not misplaced. He had served his entire sea career with Esso Tankers and had retired recently as their commodore master. As a deck cadet and then navigating officer aboard VLCCs and their larger ULCC cousins, since leaving nautical college he had been promoted along with the capacity of the ships. When the 30,000 tonner was a 'large' tanker Captain Agnew had served upon this, up to command of their 500,000 tonners. As I would discover, this wide experience with diverse tanker officers and crews had bestowed an ability to formulate pretty accurate assessments of fellow mariners. It seemed word of mouth between company directors' had led him to apply to Chandris Tankers of England even before drawing his first payment of Esso, Merchant Navy Officers' and State pensions. He told me later as we became more acquainted that, until the ship experienced a later flag change, he was paying his entire Chandris salary in UK income tax!

Living ashore was inconvenient but palatable. The Odense Steel Shipbuilding Company provided us with a large house sufficient to take the captain, navigating officers and our eight engineering officers, sparks and a chief steward each in separate rooms, but sharing communal showers and toilets. Until the ship was habitable, the steward was expected to keep the hostel accommodation clean, including linen changes, while we officers worked aboard the tanker during the day. He also liaised with the ship's agent to provide food for the evening meal and a varied light lunch of sandwiches and assorted 'goodies' plus a battery of vacuum flasks that we took aboard each morning, although the company provided him with a non-resident afternoon cook.

My next surprise came the following day. Following a leisurely breakfast, I joined the others to climb into a minibus for the drive to our ship. Turning the corner, my first close-up impression of *Rania Chandris* was again of absolute sheer size. We drove alongside a solid cliff of black steel hull that dwarfed the surrounding sheds and seemed to continue into eternity. A makeshift lift took us slowly upwards on the lengthy journey to the main deck. Leaving the lift forward of the manifolds, I was confronted by a maze of massive blue-grey piping and steel-grey deck, above which grew an enormous expanse of white accommodation adorned with strident red 2m-high NO SMOKING notices splattered across the front. My face doubtless expressed the complete awe swirling within me for I caught a lopsided grin (but no further comments) from Captain Agnew. My thoughts refroze at the idea of taking this monster to sea and learning and working with the functions of the pipework: the very notions seemed preposterous. I felt totally insignificant, caught up in casual chatter of the other officers as we walked alongside the four 5m-high main cargo pipes and catwalk containing red fire monitors towards our new home.

The combined wheelhouse/chartroom was on the seventh deck. Navigating officers cabins were on the sixth deck, or D deck, and the engineering officers, including the chief, berthed on the fifth, C, deck. An internal lift took us to our deck, where my cabin was on the port side of the lift sandwiched between Paul, the second officer, and Tim, the first, who was berthed in the pilot's cabin directly opposite the lift entrance and access to the wheelhouse companionway. Derek's larger suite of rooms

Leaving the jetty lift and walking from gangway towards accommodation block presented an impressive view. (Ray Solly)

was on the opposite port side to the master. On very rare occasions when we berthed a pilot overnight, he was placed either in one of the single cadet cabins or the ship's hospital. Ben, the radio officer, and his shack were on the after part of the port side. Captain Agnew chattered away happily as he pointed out my cabin. He was plainly in his element! After my very compact quarters aboard dry-cargo vessels I was astounded at the large size of this accommodation. The cabin was airy and pleasingly furnished with light-blue Formica bulkheads, a matching soft-seated chair and settee (which traditionally was called a 'day bed') and a wide double-berthed bunk. A massive desk adjacent to a large window looked singularly lonely adorned with merely a telephone and angle-bracketed lamp. Just inside the cabin door was a cubicle containing a toilet and shower. The master's suite of rooms was next along on the starboard side looking forward, with two cadets' cabins, study and toilet running aft, although we did not carry either deck or engineer trainees on this voyage.

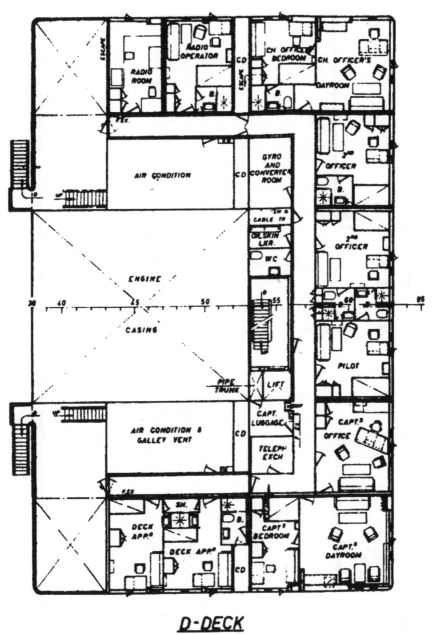

D-DECK

The disposition of cabins on the navigating officers' 'D' deck.

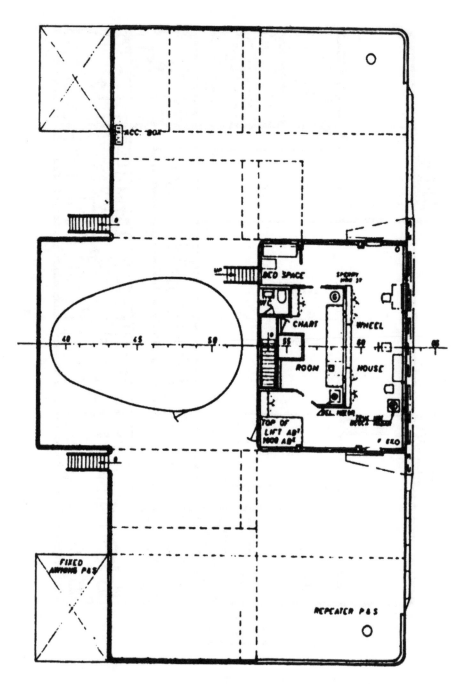

A combined wheelhouse and chartroom disposition typical of many VLCCs.

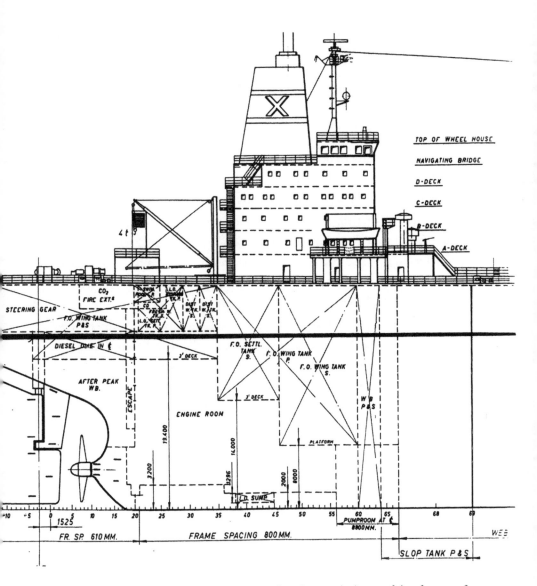

A drawing from the ship's plans of Rania Chandris *showing the layout of the after part of the vessel. The height from keel to top of funnel was 210ft (64m).*

Glancing across the main deck from my cabin windows, my recent apprehension returned, batting backwards and forwards like the proverbial yo-yo! I reflected how restricted were views from the wheelhouse of my dry-cargo vessels and again pondered how this unbelievable monster would react under her helm. My jumbled reverie was broken by Derek giving the customary perfunctory knock, as he popped through the open door and casually dropped two ship's plans onto my desk for me to study and retain. One was a General Arrangement (GA) plan that gave full deck, accommodation and tank layout details, and the other was a Capacity plan – and with each I was to become all too familiar. He later gave me ship's copies of lifesaving appliances (LSA) plans, for which I would be directly responsible, along with deck, sounding pipe and other plans of the vessel.

Before settling to studying these, I went up a deck into the wheelhouse to satisfy my curiosity concerning the ship's navigational gear. There were no shocks here and, having previously instinctively noticed two radar scanners while glancing at the accommodation block, saw our two sets: a conventional Decca Relative-Motion job on the starboard side of the main control panel, plus a very sophisticated Marconi True Motion 'all singing and dancing' computerised anti-collision set. The chart table was defronted by a thick black curtain, to restrict the shaded light to the chartroom area and prevent this interfering with keeping a proper lookout in the wheelhouse. This quick glance also captured the ubiquitous Mark 21 Decca Navigator and Marconi Lodestone Direction Finder common to virtually all ocean-going ships. The familiar layout of navigational instruments, traditionally poised angle bracket lamp over the chart area with its subduing light switch, and standard two chronometers helped me feel more a part of this colossal adventure.

As I looked at the 'new to me' portable VHF communication sets and charging panel, for which I would be responsible, on the port after side I heard the door open and, glancing around, saw Captain Agnew entering the wheelhouse. We exchanged a few more 'breaking the ice' pleasantries, during which he explained that our main deck was coloured grey for two reasons: not only because it was a working surface, but also to ease the strain on the eyesight of us navigators. The sun's glare on a white deck had

Contrasting shots taken from the bridge of a dry-cargo ship and a VLCC. The uncluttered view of the latter considerably assisted lookout duties associated with watch-keeping. (Both Ray Solly)

Views of the wheelhouse and chartroom aboard the VLCC Mangelia. *(Shell International Trading and Shipping)*

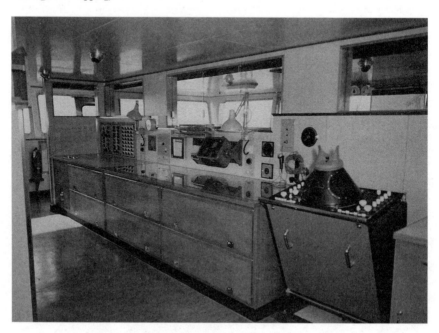

led to a number of officers in the past having been forced to give up their professions due to defects introduced into their vision by these previously impractical white decks. While he was saying some companies preferred instead to paint their decks green, Derek popped in through the port-side bridge wing door to say he had dumped some suitable gear in my cabin from a recently opened container, and wanted me to walk around the main deck 'not only to familiarise yourself with all and sundry but to make yourself useful and take a stick of chalk, your working notebook and pen to jot down any jobs that seemed necessary for reporting to the dockyard'. He had given me a pretty wide brief so before venturing onto the main deck I stopped off in my cabin to find I was now the proud recipient of two boiler suits, a hard hat, some heavy-duty working shoes and a yellow spark-free torch for use later in the cargo tanks.

Suitably equipped, and frankly not having a clue what exactly I was supposed to be looking for and reporting, I set out onto the main deck. It was not long before I found out. My meanderings soon revealed that an entrance to a main tank for a portable Butterworth cleaning machine had over it a protruding piece of metal from a nearby pipe support. It had not been cut away properly, so would prevent the machine being lowered. Once focused on the possibilities open to my piece of chalk and notebook, my enthusiasm knew no bounds, so before long a number of similar obstructions and overlaps had been marked and recorded. My afternoon inspections entailed entering number two centre cargo tank, easily the largest on the ship. Climbing over the coaming and descending the ladder leading 94.2ft (or 28.4m) to the bottom was an eerie feeling.

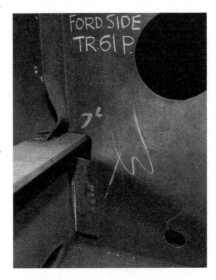

Damage to inner tanks discovered following an inspection prior to handing over the tanker. (Shell ITS)

A series of vertically staggered landings offered a chance to examine the tank construction. Obviously I had seen pictures in seamanship books of tank interiors but it was interesting to see for myself the girders and brackets, and afterwards swash bulkheads in the wing tanks. Light shone feebly in beams from the tank top entrance and openings for Butterworth machines so the scene was not one of gloomy darkness but was painted in almost spectral light, enhancing the cathedral-like atmosphere.

This view reminded me that following my acceptance by Chandris, and just two days prior to joining, fired by the dimensions of this ship I had taken an opportunity after visiting a much-loved maiden aunt in Canterbury to pop into the cathedral for a chat with their clerk of works. He told me the nave of his cathedral was 80ft high (24.5m), while the length covered 517ft (157.7m). It was 70ft wide (21.4m), while Bell Harry Tower reached a staggering 234ft (71.3m). Once aboard in my cabin, with a few quiet moments after lunch before setting out on my next adventure, I studied the dimensions of *Rania Chandris* from the GA plan and made some interesting comparisons. My ship, at 1,140ft overall length, was not only twice the length of the cathedral, but exceeded twice that length by 100 feet. (For those who know Canterbury, were the supertanker placed where the cathedral is sited, with stern at the east end of the church pointing in a north-westerly direction, the bows would extend beyond the Marlowe theatre.) At 170.4ft beam, the ship was two-and-a-half times wider than the cathedral and, with a moulded depth of 94.2ft, was 14ft higher than the nave. Bell Harry Tower was just 24ft higher than the 64m distance from keel to funnel top. Our largest cargo tank, number two centre, measured 207ft long, 71.3ft wide and 94.2ft deep but, at 306ft long, around 130ft wide and 55ft high, it would still be a squeeze by length to fit one of our smaller cathedrals (say Rochester) into this cavernous hole.

Reaching the bottom of this particular tank among the stringers, I started examining the structure. Not only was the pipe work studied, while wondering where this came from and went to, but possible faults were eagerly sought for entering into my book. In order to reach the next section of the tank I had to clamber through manholes that

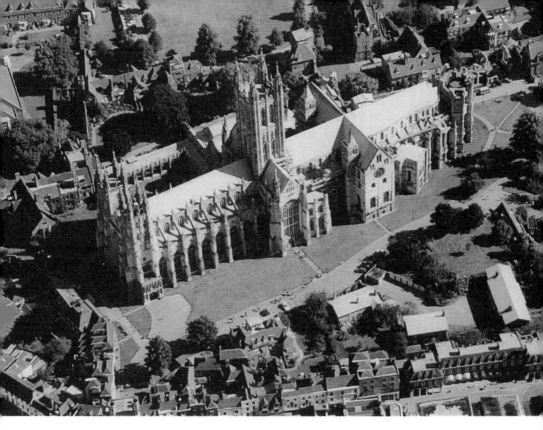

The Rania Chandris *was more than twice the length of Canterbury Cathedral. (Bill Oates and Judges of Hastings)*

separated the various tank verticals. All too soon, after contorting through an endless series, it became second nature to twist my body by putting through one leg first, following this with a bent trunk, and finishing off with the remaining leg. A number of buckled plates were soon noticed, justifying some satisfyingly extra entries. Moving around the cargo tanks quickly became second nature, although clambering up ladders, until my metabolism readjusted and I could shin up these with the agility of a (long-lost) teenager, was initially exhausting. I needed every landing to regain my breath. My deck sojourn took me up to the fo'c'sle along both decks and the catwalk, which was a legally required safety passage leading from accommodation to right forward. The distance to the jetty from the fo'c'sle head was awesome and, climbing onto the first red fire monitor, my view aft seemed almost to stretch into infinity!

I was confronted during my initial inspection of the main deck by a complete maze of interlocking pipes, the function and destinations of which were a complete mystery, a situation soon to change! (Both Ray Solly)

Conversations over dinner that evening were certainly animated. I listened carefully and tried to take in the comparisons discussed of technical differences found between our ship and previous tankers upon which the others had served. This was helped enormously by careful study afterwards of my GA plan, which helped the process of me making some kind of sense regarding the functions of the pipe work, separate ballast system and cargo leads.

Visiting the cargo control room and pump room with Paul led to an introduction of functions and operation regarding the numerous valves and levers and a rough idea of how these interrelated with those in the square deck boxes. For variety, I used an instrument designed to test the thickness of paint on the deck plates and compared these readings with the maker's manual in the mate's office. I also visited the few areas in the chief engineer's domain that shared responsibilities with our deck department. These included the steering gear compartment, and wandering around

The catwalk of any tanker was a legal requirement, facilitating safe passage when the vessel experienced heavy weather and the main deck was partially under water. (Shell ITS)

I looked in on the pintle with its series of delicately slender lubricating pipes on top of the rudder. The distance along the propeller shaft seemed to go on forever, while the six-cylinder 23,000shp main steam turbine engine towered through four decks.

One job that was instructive, but not overly enjoyable, was inspecting the web framework of the ballast tanks aft. This entailed taking my torch and stuffing my boiler suit pockets with spare bulbs, batteries and a ball of stuff similar to strong twine, plus a packet of white chalk. I had to lower myself through the rat hole on the main deck aft of the accommodation

The accommodation end of the catwalk showing the first of nine raised fire monitors situated along the main deck. (Ray Solly)

on the port side, descending various layers through a system of horizontal deck rat holes and vertical bulkhead manholes. I had tied one end of my ball of string to the entrance and made my way back with a series of chalk arrows, unrolling the string as I went. My mnemonic 'arrow heads point to safety' helped keep a sense of direction in pitch darkness. It also prevented any rising panic, so helping me to retain my sanity. Certainly, so far as I could ascertain all was in order, but it was with a sense of unrestrained joy that I climbed upwards, following my chalk and twine trail back to the normality of the main deck. The task had taken me over two hours and the experience was totally disorientating. In fact, it proved one of the loneliest jobs I would ever undertake in my life. I was not sorry to learn that Paul had simultaneously inspected the starboard-side tanks …

* * *

Left: *A four-ram steering motor found on many VLCCs was electro-hydraulically operated and when full helm hard over was applied from the wheelhouse could turn the ship's rudder 35 degrees port to starboard in around thirty seconds. (Clarke-Chapman)*

Below: *Testing the emergency hand-steering gear by using local push buttons fitted in the steering flat, essential during any breakdown. (BP plc)*

Access to the after ballast tank was through a rat hole in the main deck situated by the after accommodation. (BP plc)

It was with considerable relief that we received the yard's blessing to move into our cabins. Although ashore for only four days, life in the hostel had proved more tiresome than anything else for after all, looking ahead, we were taking a ship away to sea in her natural element, not a block of buildings.

By the end of ten days living aboard *Rania Chandris* a strange feeling of familiarity immersed me. Captain Agnew's 'cutting the vessel down to size' theory began to cut in and I found myself relaxing with my duties and beginning to feel at one with the ship. In that respect the VLCC and I signed a peace treaty but, for some indefinable reason, irritatingly, a certain apprehension remained concerning handling the vessel during navigational watches. I could not reason why this should be for, after all, I was not on my first voyage as an officer, having already clocked up a few years at sea 'in full and effective charge of a watch for not less than eight hours out of every twenty-four', as my various watch-keeping certificates confirmed.

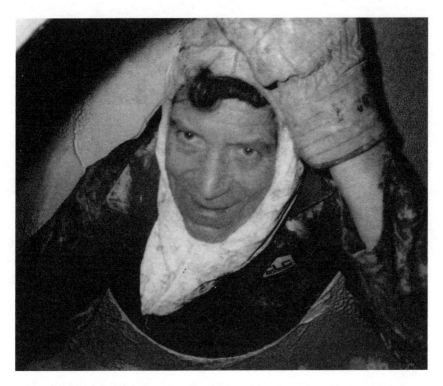

Entering and inspecting the various levels of ballast tanks port and starboard aft required certain agility. (Both Jotun Marine Coatings)

Service pipes ran the length of the vessel carrying water, foam and steam essential to running equipment on the fo'c'sle and along the main deck. (Ray Solly)

As I settled, so continued the lengthy process of learning the function of all lines and systems on board what I now regarded as 'my ship'! I noticed service pipes leaving the under tunnel from the engine room to emerge on deck slightly abaft the ladder from 'A' deck to the port side leading to the catwalk. There were ten service pipes running the length of the ship carrying the mains fire water, foam pipe both with leadings to the fire monitors and separate outlets for portable hoses, heating coil exhaust return, main exhaust return, main steam pipe (which was inevitably discoloured), Butterworth line for tank cleaning equipment, fuel oil, diesel oil, a compressed air pipe, and electrical conduit. On the other side of the catwalk ran the four main cargo pipes and ballast lines, which terminated amidships at the shore manifolds. At the extreme end of the vessel forward of the foremast, port and starboard windlasses and warping winches, was the entrance to the bosun's store. I was initially intrigued by the tall white high-velocity ventilation valve mounted on a pedestal. Opening the gauge spark arrester whilst discharging cargo prevented the

A high-velocity ventilation valve outside the entrance to the bosun's stores and forward ballast tank were hallmarks of an early-stage VLCC. (Ray Solly)

deck from being drawn downwards, and closing whilst loading allowed volatile cargo hydrocarbon gas mixtures to be expelled safely from the tanks. These actions became automatic until the ship was fitted with an Inert Gas system (IGS), which channelled and cleaned exhaust gas from the ship's funnel as a neutral gas into the cargo tanks.

The day after the momentous move on board *Rania Chandris* saw our ratings joining the vessel. The complete crew had been flown from the UK after being recruited from numerous Shipping Federation offices across the country. Captain Branch had co-ordinated their arrival at Heathrow to join a charter flight. We officers were enjoying a morning break when their coach arrived alongside the gangway. Apart from sailing with European ratings on coastal trips (a very different kind of sea animal) I had sailed previously only with deep-sea companies employing Asian catering crews from Goa and deck/engineer ratings from India and Pakistan. So it was with particular interest that I watched our crowd working under the mate's, second engineer's and steward's supervision as they sorted out their gear for loading via the midships derrick and, in small parties, entered our limited-capacity lift to arrive on the main deck. I glanced sideways at Paul, quietly assessing his reactions based on his wider deep-sea experience with British ratings aboard Shell Tankers. Certainly, my first impressions were rather guarded (to put things mildly) and I wondered if some were roaring drunk, for most seemed at least to be glowing brightly. Paul's passive expression did not show any surprise or shock so, crew control not being my direct concern, I decided to keep an open mind and see how events might transpire.

Over coffee in the lounge after supper I listened to a mixed variety of views across all departments concerning others' first impressions of our lads, gaining the idea they were an uncomplicated typical crew. I did not mention my thoughts about some being possibly drunk, deeming it perhaps wise to keep my own counsel.

As the officers' steward brought my breakfast in our dining saloon the following morning my reflections regarding our crew deepened. They seemed to have settled in well and already varying personalities were emerging among those with whom I would have to work directly. Our pump man, for instance, was grossly overweight but possessed of a lively sense of humour. This was just as well because, coming from a smaller tanker, he soon found going up and down cargo, ballast tanks and the pump room immensely draining. We discussed with Derek our very real concerns that he 'might have a heart attack, or stroke or something', but practically there was very little we could do as his tasks had to be done and there was no senior cadet we could assign to help with his essential duties. All parties, however, seemed to enjoy the nickname 'Tanks' I bestowed upon him.

Geordie, the duty quartermaster assigned to my watch, was another lively character, but our first meeting was not particularly fortuitous. As the bosun, or chief petty officer, in charge of the deck ratings introduced us and we made eye contact, something in my AB's manner rang a few alarm bells. He immediately plunged into a repertoire of jokes that seemed inappropriate during a first … I found myself using the word … encounter. His whole demeanour impressed as something of an act.

I was left wondering why and already questioning the substance of the actual man and how he would act while on watch. The bosun also seemed far too much of a 'hail fellow well met' and, as they wandered off, I decided again to keep my thoughts to myself and see how things might transpire. 'Chippy', our carpenter, the second chief petty officer, appeared as an unassuming man of middle age but seemingly quiet disposition. In fact, we responded favourably to each other immediately, leaving me breathing a sigh of relief.

CHAPTER TWO

SURPRISES ALONG THE WAY

Just two days later came the exciting news from our agent that trials had been arranged the following Monday and Tuesday, with Wednesday laid aside for any overlaps. There was certainly a buzz in the conversation that evening over supper.

On the glorious sunny and calm day, no time was wasted for at 0800 hrs prompt our Danish pilot boarded the vessel with a complete set of officers and ratings. Our chief, working with his Danish counterpart, had already made ready the main engines and auxiliary machinery and, as technically (and legally) the ship still belonged to the shipbuilders, their Danish ensign was hoisted at the stern. But with a host of tugs made fast fore and aft and three in attendance, a triumphant blast from our whistle encouraged *Rania Chandris* to ease herself slowly away from the jetty.

Admittedly, there was little for me to learn initially as I watched my Danish opposite number perform the traditional third officer duties in the wheelhouse, because these were pretty standard procedures aboard all ships: testing the helm, hoisting appropriate flags, opening a brand new movement book, liaising with the duty engineer and synchronising clocks, telegraph control and telephones to all departments, and keeping an eye on the steering. As we were on what would become my eight-to-twelve watch, I felt far more comfortable with the positively responsible attitude shown by my quartermaster standing by his Danish equivalent.

After entering the Kattegat and clearing main shipping lanes, we belted around the seas putting everything through its paces, or as Captain Agnew described our antics, 'testing everything that was testable on the ship'. I watched him and the pilot handle this enormous vessel and found it extremely interesting and professionally encouraging to discuss and witness such things as turning circles, timings for ship response to helm and engines, and numerous technical niceties.

Once I was relieved to go on deck with my opposite number, we went everywhere and watched everything. The Danish ratings under their officers checked all fire monitors and portable hoses, both with water and foam and, as maintenance and operation of all LSA equipment would be part of my specific responsibilities, I was invited to handle one of the monitors and assess swing limits laterally and vertically. All cargo gear was run to capacity, including manifold connections, pumps and valves, and all cargo and ballast tanks were filled beyond capacity so that sea water ran over the main deck. Each docking winch and the windlass was tested. Butterworth tank cleaning machines were put through their paces, but the two 23-ton anchors were lowered only as we came to our anchorage following successful completion of the trials.

At the invitation of our chief engineer, I spent some time below in the engine room watching the main steam turbine engine working smoothly, and saw the testing of both generators and all other auxiliary machinery. Then I wandered into the pump room and witnessed all the cargo and ballast valves in full operation as we again flooded to capacity all cargo and ballast tanks, allowing water to run freely over the deck, before emptying these.

We returned at the end of a couple of days to anchor off Copenhagen, with the master and chief engineer pronouncing their satisfaction with 'most things in most respects'. Once papers were signed, Chandris Tankers of England, with some pride, took formal delivery of *Rania Chandris* as the latest addition to its expanding VLCC fleet. It was with a sense of achievement that the Red Ensign was formally hoisted to the jack mast astern. We felt the ship was finally ours.

On any ship's trials, all equipment and gear is subjected to rigorous testing prior to handing over the vessel from builders to owners. Here the forward fire monitor is tested with high-pressure foam prior to being cleaned with sea water. (Shell ITS)

To the chagrin of Sparks and the engineering officers, apart from the chief, second and two thirds, all deck officers were invited to the handing over ceremony and sumptuous dinner party later that evening held in a prestigious Copenhagen hotel. The chairman and board of directors' popped over from Piraeus and it was good to touch base once more and discuss my progress with Captain Branch, plus meet a few officials from the London office. Drinks flowed freely as we settled to *le banquet extraordinaire*, as French gourmets would doubtless have described our lavish meal.

★ ★ ★

We had spent eleven days working on board, which was entered into a special section of our Discharge 'A' books as 'standing by', allowing the days to be included as 'sea time' for those with certificates of competency still to finalise. For much of the three days until we sailed on our maiden voyage, I was busy on a multitude of jobs. These included helping Captain Agnew by compiling a crew list from our collective Discharge 'A' books and then preparing lifeboat manning schedules and drawing up groups of ratings, each under an officer, for emergency drills, including parties of seven or eight sailors who worked under the three deck officers according to orders from the chief officer. These drills always took place immediately after lifeboat drill had been completed and covered three different tasks: regular testing of foam monitors, or the water hoses, or a number of smoke helmet and stretcher drills occurred in various parts of the ship. These were discussed later with Derek. I set Geordie and another quartermaster assigned to me the task of splicing lights to all lifebuoys, leaving me free to organise a range of LSA equipment. There were various forms that had to be completed for official Lloyd's Register and company purposes, in the midst of continuing a lengthy process of learning the functions of numerous deck pipes.

Previously, when joining any ship, all systems had been in place and up and running, so I had not realised that starting a vessel from scratch involved so many detailed jobs.

At 1600 hrs, two days after arriving back in Denmark, the pilot joined the vessel and I was sent by Captain Agnew to call the carpenter, go for'rard and weigh the starboard anchor, and then stand by with him on the fo'c'sle for departure from Helsingør bound for Las Palmas, where we would bunker. I took one of the VHF sets that I had previously charged and tested, finding this novelty a vast improvement over racing to the telephone in the eyes of the ship every time the bridge wished to communicate a message for'rard. This invariably occurred at an awkward moment while berthing alongside and, when there was no cadet to answer the thing, was something of a nuisance. As things stood now, the duty mate in the wheelhouse and I were in constant communication – in this case the chief officer – merely by clicking a button. Following the compactness of a fo'c'sle on dry-cargo ships and especially coasters, the massive space around which I moved and the size of the windlass and all gear still remained awesome, as did the distance to the accommodation block aft. It was 1745 before we were stood down, just in time for supper, but the time was well spent chatting casually with Chips, strengthening a growing friendship founded, it seemed, on mutual respect.

At 1950, I went through the wheelhouse door to relieve Tim. Although the pilot was still on board, I used the Decca Swedish Chain 10B for checking and fixing the vessel's position, afterwards during my four-hour stint making frequent course alterations to the automatic pilot as we passed Arnholt light vessel while proceeding on passage between numbers three and seven fairway buoys. The master occasionally popped into the wheelhouse, but generally the watch proceeded well with the vessel moving easily in a calm sea and low swell. My quartermaster kept a visual lookout on the starboard bridge wing for most of the time, reporting to myself or the pilot passing vessels efficiently and as necessary. Other than phoning the chief steward arranging for collection of the bridge box each morning, and then Paul agreeing his customary pre-watch shake by phone at 2340 and 2355, the watch passed quietly and well. The distances between bridge wings across the wide wheelhouse, which extended the length of one coaster upon which I served, and that forward, remained something of a shock every time I moved from chart table to steering console. As darkness closed in, the other thing I found disturbing initially was the sight of the minute foremast indicator light in the rear of that light confirming that the thing was still working. Being comparatively low down, until I became accustomed to it, my glances forward meant it hit my vision and 'gave me a bit of a turn', as I described it to Paul, by looking like a distant ship's anchor or stern light, dead ahead.

Communication between the duty
officer aft or forward and the master
or pilot on the bridge was essential.
The process was much facilitated
by the introduction of VHF sets,
replacing the necessity of having a
cadet standing by the telephones.
(BP plc)

Rania Chandris *freshly painted and ready to go proceeds on her maiden voyage. Under a different name, this VLCC served companies associated with the Chandris Lines in Piraeus for the next twenty-two years. (Odense Steel Shipyard)*

I was called by the officers' steward just after 0715 with a welcome cup of tea and in adequate time to have a shower, come to, and pop in for a substantial breakfast prior to going into the wheelhouse for my first solo watch at 0800. After going through the usual handing over ritual and mentioning we had dropped the Danish pilot one hour earlier off Skagen pilot station, Tim shot off to a welcome bunk, leaving me aware of the door closing with a gentle, almost subdued, click.

It is amazing how life sometimes offers its minions a sense of déjà vu moments. For suddenly I recalled my very first solo bridge watch after qualifying as a navigating officer some seven years previously when first being left alone by the captain and how – surprisingly – my own and every other ship continued along predetermined tracks perfectly safely without any histrionics. Now, standing alone by the steering console, my 'moment of previous apprehension' arrived, accompanied not by concern but a surprising sense of familiarity. The gyrocompass clicked quietly, compensating for fluctuations while maintaining our course of 350 degrees (True); the two radar sets whirred unobtrusively, the VHF chattered animatedly and my quartermaster coughed just outside the starboard door where I had placed him to keep his lookout in coastal waters, particularly for other ships but also points of navigational interest and any potential obstructions in the water. Sparks popped in, dropped off a weather report and commented casually on some incidental happening, before returning to his shack. Life continued normally: land did not suddenly appear under our bows or another ship suddenly alter course leading into a collision situation.

As I navigated the vessel through the Skagerrak and later into the North Sea, the realisation soon came that the supertanker indeed handled similarly to any other class of ship. She certainly required more thought before taking any action to alter course as she was initially slow to respond to her helm, but once she gained slight momentum and answered she came around fairly quickly and required counter-helm almost immediately to bring her up and regain control. Very often during this (and subsequent) watches I took Captain Agnew's advice by knocking her off auto-pilot, or 'Mad Mike' as it was universally and colloquially called, to steer her manually, testing this reaction to her helm and so physically gaining a 'feel' for the vessel.

Two hours later, at 1000, I checked the chronometers against the Greenwich time signal, noticing one was completely accurate while the other was four seconds fast, following this with a routine change of tele-motor systems after a previous agreement with the chief engineer, and noticed signals from the Decca Swedish 10B chain were already fading as we lost range. A moment's experimentation determined it was too early for the English 5B chain to be detected so I used radar to fix the ship's position. Captain Agnew popped onto the bridge around 1000, so I sent my AB below for a twenty-minute 'smoke-oh' as the steward arrived with a welcome coffee tray and plate of biscuits set up for the master and myself. Taking that first appreciative sip and glancing at me over his cup, he smiled gently and asked if 'all is well?' I smiled an understanding affirmative regarding his subtle ambiguity, confirming that while his ship would never cease to stagger me by its dimensions, 'I was at this stage feeling confident and becoming increasingly competent at handling her!'

I was very impressed with the all-singing, all-dancing Marconi main radar. When the main radar was used at its lowest half-mile setting in the very calm seas experienced, it was fascinating to watch the 'V' wake of a gull taking off from the water as the ship approached too closely for its comfort. The outline of the ship was etched clearly, which came in very handy later for the master and pilots docking the supertanker in conditions of restricted visibility. The automatic plotting facility was acceptably accurate and gave a useful indication of the closest point of approach, time and distance of passing ships. This was a luxury I had never experienced before but did not regret the absence of the need to plot targets manually either onto the screen with a sharply pointed chinagraph pencil, or the alternatives of a paper 'spider' diagram or wooden/plastic RAS plotting board. This was the only option available in those days, but was far from accurate. Invariably, the task was trying to reduce a 12-mile radar screen to a diagram about 18in in diameter, leading inevitably to a mere indication, thus substantiating the well-known fact that radar was merely an aid to navigation. The other problem, of course, arose when a choice of targets presented itself, as this manual system could cope only with one plot at a time. At least the input effort did produce an indication of a potential collision situation. By far more useful was the manual placing of a bearing cursor onto a target: if the target did not move away appreciably but 'moved down the cursor' it indicated the potential of a collision.

★ ★ ★

We carried a guarantee chief engineer from the Lindo yard on our maiden voyage, along with six Finnish fitters who, as the chief officer gradually flooded and then emptied our ballast tanks, attached zinc anodes at varying vertical levels to slow the processes of corrosion. It was quite interesting watching the latter fitting their rubber boat, anodes and welding gear into the tank top.

The next day set patterns that would become norms while the vessel was at sea or anchor watch. My two four-hour watches were interspersed by taking sights around 0900 hrs and then, along with Paul, taking a local time noon sight. Afterwards, I had lunch followed by two or three hours of deck work either with Derek or the master. What was not the norm was a run-in with Geordie, my deck man! As lookout duties were not exactly all-embracing during daylight hours in good visibility, I set him regular tasks of sweeping and washing down the wheelhouse, chartroom and bridge wing areas, and then cleaning all the brass work. Afterwards I turned him to with the bosun. On the first occasion after the cleaning and washing down had been done to my satisfaction, I suddenly noticed his absence. He popped back with the Brasso but suddenly disappeared again. When he finally emerged, I asked him what exactly were the problems encountered over such a simple job of brass cleaning. Listening to a long rambling explanation, I lost patience, telling him that I had done this job frequently when a cadet and knew perfectly well how long it should take, including the step edges on both external ladders. Fixing him with a steely eye, I told him if the job were not completed within the next twenty min-utes to my satisfaction, then I would report him to the chief officer and arrange for his replacement by another AB. I coped extremely well with the look of malignant gloom cast in my direction, but he worked with such a will that Captain Agnew, popping along for his morning coffee and chat, looked at him with focused attention and then at me. He obviously guessed we had exchanged some kind of love talk because we both enjoyed exchanging a humorous glance, making further comments superfluous.

Off Dogger Bank, a slight technical problem was found with the Decca Arkas Autopilot during Tim's morning watch when the thing suddenly emitted an unexpectedly piercing shriek, momentarily fright-ening him and his quartermaster out of their wits: the mechanical/ electrical pilot had veered the ship beyond the manually set fixed limit of 10 degrees from her course line. Tim solved the problem by resetting it, and later in the day Norman, our sparks, 'cleaned a few contacts', which fixed the thing.

One of the daily duties of the quartermaster assigned to the morning watch was cleaning the wheelhouse deck and brass work and then washing down. (BP plc)

Bridge watch-keeping consisted essentially of ensuring the vessel kept to her course line and lookout duties for other ships and potential collision hazards. Using all available means meant identifying targets visually and by radar, with the next step invariably checking through binoculars and where necessary discussing any situation with a colleague. (BP plc)

I had always found the Dover Strait and its approaches extremely interesting stretches of water and this trip was no exception, greatly enhanced in such a large vessel by paying much closer attention (as I had previously guessed) to potential problems arising from depth of water under the keel. We celebrated our first trip in these waters manoeuvring *Rania Chandris* through dense fog before, during and after navigating the deep-water channel that passed Varne light vessel down our starboard side. My role was to operate the main radar on the 6-mile range and report to the master time, range, bearing and closest point of approach of other potential collision-situation ships. He identified these on the 3-mile range of our secondary set, followed them down, and gave alterations to our course where necessary to my quartermaster. I also popped a dot on the chart every thirty minutes or so conveniently sandwiched between radar plotting. Decca Navigator English Chain 5B invariably displayed excellent results, so once the readings were crossed with radar ranges and bearings, and confirmed where possible by visual bearings, we obtained reliable position fixes in these confined waters.

On each Saturday, we followed standard tanker practice of exercising fire and boat drills. One of the two boats was invariably lowered to the embarkation deck, checking simultaneously the smooth running of all gear, including the motor. I was in the master's boat, but as he was nearly always occupied in the wheelhouse co-ordinating the various activities, I ran the boat, although leaving much of the routine lowering and raising to the bosun. I simply checked off the crew against the list and encouraged them where necessary to wear life jackets correctly. This was particularly relevant with the new deck and catering boys, one of each of whom was assigned to my boat.

The first use by all parties of fire hoses led to another slight run-in with Geordie, my quartermaster. By intercepting an indefinably quick glance he shot at the first-trip deck boy, I guessed that something was coming, so was not particularly surprised when he asked me very casually if I wanted him to roll the hose we had just used and stow this away. My terse blistering delivered in quietly calm but calculated tones suggesting that

The officer's duty during essential weekly boat drills aboard tankers was to check all crew were present and that life jackets were being worn correctly. Invariably, the boats were lowered to the main deck. In the early days of tanker trading, although these drills were carried out responsibly, they were otherwise quite informal. In subsequent voyages all crew were issued with hard hats and told to wear appropriate long-sleeved clothing. (BP plc)

Following the boat drill, emergency stations afterwards included one of a number of drills. Here the crew were supervised in running water hose tests. (BP plc)

a man of his experience ought to know the hose had to be dried before being stowed away, opened the deck boy's eyes considerably, and left my QM looking decidedly bashful, as well it might. I could never tell when and under what circumstances he would 'try it on', as Derek described his antics after overhearing our exchange. Later, over a cup of afternoon tea, the mate asked me 'are you quite comfortable with him', accepting with a rueful exchange of grins my assurance that, 'Yes, I feel quite up to handling whatever tricks this particular AB might devise!'

★ ★ ★

My after-lunch deck work had developed into a complete variety of interesting duties. Initially, during the mornings after washing down, I set Geordie the continuing task of fixing lights to buoys. These he completed competently and devoid of histrionics. I worked in the forward and after-peak store lockers with the bosun and pump man, helped Derek in the cargo control room and manipulated external deck valves while exchanging ballast water between tanks as the fitters completed their task, worked on soundings with chippy, and continued the task of measuring paint thicknesses on just about every area where the latter had been applied. The tank measuring gauges indicating ullages in cargo tanks were already causing concerns by sticking, so in optimistic preparation for when we were loaded, Captain Agnew and I worked a system designed to encourage them to function normally, although this would prove an ongoing task for much of my time aboard the ship. In preparation for future promotion, I helped Paul with an endless run of chart corrections, including running repairs to various publications as amendments to these were received on the ship.

Ullages in the tanks were measured quite accurately from gauges fitted to the cargo tank tops, although occasionally these had an annoying habit of sticking, necessitating hand measuring using 90ft of measuring tape and a weight. (Ray Solly)

Taking morning and noon sights became a regular practice once out of sight of land or the range of an excellently accurate Decca Navigator system. The second and third officers invariably compared readings prior to reducing their calculations and giving the ship's position. (BP plc)

Signals from the Decca ceased to be reliable and had been lost completely just before entering the Bay of Biscay, so for the last two days all deck officers had commenced taking appropriate celestial observations, following these by Mercator sailing calculations, and compass azimuths and amplitudes. Having only a couple of months earlier taken the full range of sights aboard my dry-cargo vessel, no problems were experienced with these, but the height of eye above sea level on this monster of 110ft differed considerably from the modest 50ft or so on dry-cargo ships.

At 0820 hrs I picked up Gran Canary (rather humorously) at 50 miles, just outside the 48-mile radar range ring, on the physical edge of the set. More realistically, I was able to take a ranging bearing on La Isleta light at 24-mile range just over an hour later. By 1000 hrs it was 1.5 miles away and, as the master entered the wheelhouse, I rang 'stand by' on the engines in preparation for arrival alongside Las Palmas. We took the pilot on board at the civilised hour of 1147. Having met him at the pilot ladder and then delivered him to Captain Agnew, I continued customary third mate standby duties in the wheelhouse. These were carried out in a far more leisurely way than on board a smaller vessel, as the first line was not put ashore until 1238. It took the first and second officers just under two hours to take tugs and lead out moorings, bringing *Rania Chandris* in position alongside the far end of the jetty, so by 1400 hrs when my QM and I had been stood down from the wheelhouse, we went on deck and lowered the gangway and fixed a noticeboard indicating our estimated time of departure at midnight. It was then over to the engineers to load fuel, diesel and assorted lubricating oils for the forthcoming voyage.

I took advantage of an excess of mates and a limitation in duties to pop ashore with Paul to a port new to him, and to one that had not appeared on my menu for quite a few years. I had always enjoyed the heavy Spanish influence here. In fact, one of my very first seafaring souvenirs on my own maiden voyage had been a small locally crafted marquetry trinket box, which proved ideal for collar studs and cufflinks in those halcyon days of dressing for formal dinners. On this occasion we both bartered for some delicate lace presents for the lady folk in our lives. It was good to stretch our legs and have a local varied fish banquet for supper, washed down with a good couple of bottles of the local Lagosta wine, returning on board around 1900 hrs.

With our pilot and tugs ordered for 0200, it was just after 0130 that Derek asked me to turn-to the deckhands in preparation for departure from Las Palmas. He clearly knew what he was doing and was happy to widen my experience of European tanker crews, for the entire deck

Rania Chandris *alongside the outer jetty at Las Palmas dwarfs two large deep-sea, dry-cargo vessels forward. (Ray Solly)*

crowd from bosun to both deck boys was absolutely plastered. There was not one sober man among them. I was greeted like a long-lost brother, with Bose slobbering all over me mouthing drunken pleasantries and compliments, but not over-exerting himself to rouse his lads. He clearly did not know whether he was aboard *Rania Chandris* or the *Royal Scot*, but this reception was certainly more acceptable than any attitude that might have been more aggressive.

Chips quietly and assumedly was the first to leave the crew accommodation so, after a great deal of persuasion and 'bonhomie' – false though the latter may have been – with his example before them, I managed to lead the crowd onto deck, where they were grabbed by the first and second officers before they could change their minds and assorted into their respective 'standby' groups. As it was well after departure time, the tugs were waiting patiently for someone to make them fast fore and aft, while the pilot and master, long accustomed to the vagaries of European crews, discussed trivial matters. I took my well-watered quartermaster and the first-trip deck boy to raise and dismantle the gangway as necessary, and then lower the pilot hoist on the starboard side. It was as well I had done these duties frequently as a cadet, for Geordie had a distinct look in his eye, which made it clear he was well aware that he had left me to tell them what should be done. Bowing to the inevitable, I did precisely that. But in turn I left him under no illusions regarding my thoughts.

It was 0250 before I appeared in the wheelhouse lugging the AB with me to take the helm. Tugs had already been made fast and the ship singled up fore and aft so, once the QM took the wheel and I stood by telegraphs, phones and movement book, we departed Las Palmas. It was lucky the steering console was there, otherwise Geordie might well have tumbled over. However, his experience was so extensive that he managed to obey the pilot's commands in auto-drive, although the master looked at him very directly once or twice. I did wonder whether or not I might have to step in to relieve this gibbering apology on the wheel, and steer the ship myself.

A further contretemps occurred with Geordie the next day out of Las Palmas. Since leaving Denmark he had regaled me with an endless repertoire of occasionally quite amusing but mainly pointlessly filthy jokes. As the OOW, it had always been a point of personal honour to pick up lights (especially) long before they were reported by any quartermaster, so I was surprised when he turned to me saying, 'Ship two points starboard.' As this one was neither visible through binoculars nor detected as a target on the radar, I questioned what he was reporting, only to be told the vessel in question 'was two days away'. This was the proverbial last straw. He accepted my watery smile and direct look as signs of appreciation, but was definitely not pleased by being told to 'Stop reporting rubbish' and then being placed halfway along the starboard bridge wing to keep all future evening lookout duties, including rain squalls, instead of sheltering happily inside the outer wheelhouse shelter. During the day, following his cleaning duties, I continued turning him to with the bosun – probably to the relief of each of us, although this topic was not up for discussion. He was very supportive, however, over the extensive voyage roster I introduced to call the deck boys individually in the morning and the catering boys in the evening for an hour on the wheel, so helping them towards their thirty hours of steering instruction necessary for an in-house steering certificate. I quite happily handed them over to Geordie and, in the evening, turned out the standby man to cover his lookout duties.

CHAPTER THREE

PROBLEMS AND PERSONALITIES

Four days later off Sierra Leone our watch-keeping routines were well established. I remained awed by the sheer size of the vessel seen from the wheelhouse windows but, while still full of respect, was no longer coloured by any apprehension. The sea had indeed 'cut her down to size'.

Keeping an eye through binoculars on the safety of ant-like figures that denoted the crew working on deck under the eagle eyes of their bosun, I caught sight of two fishing fleets about 15 miles ahead, ten in number off the port bow, some twenty to starboard and about 8 miles apart. There was nothing unusual about seeing deep-sea trawlers and, judging by their VHF twitter, I suspected these were probably Japanese.

Although such a common sight in any waters, their haphazard meanderings around the ocean while they tracked shoals of various fish made their courses difficult to determine accurately. So I decided to hold my course and speed until the situation clarified itself but watch their antics. They were now about 4 miles ahead and seemed to have settled on tracks slightly divergent to our own. I decided they would pass down safely roughly 2 miles to port and probably a little less to starboard of our own ship. Relaxing, I watched them quite happily holding their courses and, seeing the crew coming towards the accommodation block and glancing at the clock, realised it was coming towards the end of my watch. I knew by now Paul enjoyed his almost traditional cup of after lunch coffee, so set up our bridge tray and switched on the kettle. Then, casually looking ahead, I had a shock. My mind froze momentarily as I suddenly realised both fleets had altered course and were now on converging courses and crossing our bows dead ahead. Rapidly refocusing my mind, I mused that, with a turning circle of around 1½ miles, if a bold alteration either to port or starboard was made we could hit the nearest ones on either side. So, with drying mouth, the only feasible action was to hold my course and speed.

Captain Agnew told me later that, in the midst of a chat over lunch in the dining saloon with his senior officers, he glanced casually out of the port-side window and saw a trawler that he thought was 'a little close'. Glancing out of the starboard window, he saw two more, 'even more closely'. Forgetting all about cheese, biscuits – and plans for the garden next time home – he jumped up from his chair to see 'a veritable host of fishing boats dead ahead'. He related diving for the companionway and racing up towards the bridge 'wondering what the hell was going on aboard his ship'!

Paul, meanwhile, had entered the wheelhouse and, with mind preoccupied by the generally open waters associated with mid-ocean watch-keeping, was mentally planning his latest batch of chart corrections, when unexpectedly he saw what looked like thirty trawlers dead ahead, on various courses either side of our ship – and me standing at the steering console clearly knocking her off automatic steering and placing her onto manual. I became aware of him suddenly standing next to me asking what I wanted him to do. Suggesting he stood by the whistle and sound appropriate signals, I prepared to steer our tanker in between the boats.

The bosun instructs a deck boy on cleaning down in preparation for revarnishing a ship's rail. (Athel Line)

I was only vaguely aware of the chart-room door opening while deciding to alter to starboard and take the first of this blasted fleet down the port side. Sparks (who subconsciously I thought it was) and his weather reports suddenly seemed small fry. Telling Paul to sound one short blast on the siren, I made the first of a number of alterations to our course to starboard, and then to port, passing the first batch of boats about half-a-mile off.

While it took probably ten minutes for us to clear the fleets, for me time stood still. I was perfectly – even icily – calm in mind, felt decisively in control of making alterations to our track, and totally focused on collision avoidance. Seemingly a lifetime later, the last trawler crossed our starboard bow and, although unaware of my emotions, I felt tension draining from my body as I straightened the ill-used *Rania Chandris* back onto her course line of 143 degrees True and Gyro.

The reality of this situation suddenly hit me. I realised then how important was the captain's initial advice when joining the ship to occasionally put her onto manual steering while taking her around headlands and avoiding collisions with other ships. This had certainly paid dividends in the confidence it had given me to con her. I retained great respect for the manner and speed in which this large ship manoeuvred within arcs of 10 or 15 degrees of port-to-starboard helm.

I became aware of Paul looking at me (as well he might), and glancing behind saw Captain Agnew standing by the chart table, also affording me a very direct glance. He told me during a later review of what had happened that he wanted to see if I could sort out this mess myself, so merely observed what I did – and the effects of my immediate actions – but had stood ready to step in if it seemed necessary to do so.

It was obvious to us all that reaction had set in. I was visibly shaken. My mouth was dry, hands shaking and stomach churning. I did not feel physically sick but could not trust myself too much!

The master told me simply to write up the logbook (which I did in writing that looked as if I were suffering from an advanced form of ague), hand over the watch to Paul, and go below. Once in my cabin, I enjoyed a refreshing wash and then lay down on the day bed. I could not face lunch in the saloon and even a cup of tea and slice or two of toast in the duty mess held no attractions. The master looked in on me after an hour or so, enquiring if I was all right. I appreciated his genuine concern, but it took another hour for me to fully recover my usual equilibrium.

Later, when Captain Agnew came up for his pre-midnight trip to the bridge for a cup of thick ship's-speciality cocoa, he asked the inevitable question, 'Oh my goodness, Mr Solly. What happened this morning?'

'Well, Sir, it is really quite simple. It seems I made an error and mis-judged the situation.'

'You know what you could have done?'

'Oh yes, Captain. Perhaps I should have opened wider to starboard much earlier and left them to sort themselves out, and not become involved.'

'Yes, well. Hmm. Perhaps that is so – but if that is your assessment, as I was not present, then you'll know another time, won't you?'

I could merely concur for there did not seem much more to say, and the situation was allowed (to my relief) to die a natural death as other events happened gradually to overtake my seeming misdemeanour. At least I had learnt more about the handling capabilities and limitations of the ship, which were to stand me in good stead with future manoeu-vrings, but it was a hard lesson to have learned in that manner – even if the circumstances were of my own making.

★ ★ ★

The shipping situation paralleling the African coast remained very busy, with high densities of assorted vessels every watch (including, of course, more of those devilish trawlers). As there were few ports until we passed Mossel and Walvis Bays, most of this shipping was passing open to port, but with plenty of diverse crossing situations requiring more immediate attention and sometimes action.

I had just been relieved from my watch when we were about two days off Cape Town when the bunk light went out in my cabin just as I was settling to enjoy my near compulsive read prior to going to sleep.

I leapt out of the bunk, feeling my way to the door and, on opening this, realised only the red emergency lighting was operational. I met Captain Agnew by the steps leading to our chartroom. We both raised eyebrows at each other before I followed him to the bridge door. It seemed the ship had experienced a total power failure: we were still under way and already Paul was heading for the after deck locker to rig our oil-powered NUC, or Not Under Command, lights. I have to confess wondering what use these would be in advertising a tanker of our dimensions, but reflected even a candle would be better than nothing if we were hit and subsequently asked at a court of enquiry what action we had taken to illuminate the vessel! After even a few moments I realised there was nothing for me to do so, clearing my dismissal with the master, I returned below and again turned in. The power was out of action for around five hours, which meant the gyrocompass stopped completely, leaving us to rely on the magnetic steering compass on the monkey island with its periscope reflector leading just above the QM's line of vision. This was fine, but we were roughly 600 nautical miles (nm) abeam of St Helena and already in this area off the African continent isogonic influences were affecting the magnetic compass. In fact, my azimuth taken just prior to coming off watch before the failure had determined a deviational error of 23 degrees east, leaving our poor old magnetic the most confused piece of equipment on the ship!

We advanced the clocks one hour, which put twenty minutes on each watch. Already the weather was becoming colder and the ship had commenced pitching moderately and rolling overall about 17 degrees as we started to encounter the infamous 'Cape rollers'. These originated from storms, possibly as far away as Antarctic waters, increasing in rate until they met shallower seas around the African southern point, where they become steeper and higher. They hit the eastern and western coasts and their waves could often reach exceptional heights, and have been known to cause considerable damage to shipping in the area. I had seen photographs of a Ben Line cargo liner proudly displaying her decidedly drooping bows as evidence of their force. But at least she had survived.

The notorious Cape rollers encountered on approaching South African waters were usually quite safe to most vessels but could create a steadily uncomfortable roll, particularly on smaller ships. (BP plc)

My time checks each morning placed our latest model 'state-of-art' Quartz chronometer some twenty-two seconds slow just seventeen days into our voyage, and I pondered if somehow that also was being knocked out of its equilibrium.

A slight difficulty was experienced during the second of my weekly fire and boat drills, commonly known in the Merchant Navy since these had been introduced some decades previously as 'Board of Trade Sports'. On the second drill, Derek put my party in charge of the nearest fire monitor, with the two other mates covering the adjacent forward monitors. Unwisely, doubtless filled with some kind of bonhomie regarding the relaxed way I had settled into VLCC routines and duties, I succumbed to the request by my deck boy for him to take control of the monitor. Inevitably, which perhaps I should have foreseen, he lost control of the thing and drenched Paul's party next in line. Impressed I may have been by the force of the water jet, but this did not dampen the burst of language emanating from the soaked party forward. Even I could detect the vitriolic words floating towards us as I hastily knocked the boy out of the way, simultaneously grabbing the monitor and facing this over the port side. Not surprisingly, the remainder of my group were rolling around creased with uncontrollable laughter, a fact not missed by the unfortunates forward. It took me a while afterwards to apologise profusely to Paul's party and treat the latter to a calming drink (or two …) in the bar after supper. Geordie told me that the crew concerned nearly lynched the boy once they had changed into dry clothes.

This was not the only change I observed regarding communal relationships on board our 'happy hooker' as our voyage progressed.

We deck and engineering officers had by this time completely relaxed in each other's company. I was learning that although the tanker trades required closer inter-departmental professional co-operation than that often found aboard deep-sea, dry-cargo ships, equally as inevitably traditional 'oily water boundaries' wallowed just below the surface. This resulted in a number of 'internal political issues' remaining precisely that. Incidents that affected only mates or engineers rarely received further public airing

There were usually nine fire monitors aboard the average VLCC used for both water and foam. The range and power behind the jet from the monitors was surprisingly extensive. (Ray Solly)

but automatically 'remained under wraps' for departmental consumption only. For instance, one of the new junior engineers went through a difficult time settling into seafaring and tanker routines but this was only apparent to us on deck through a series of imperceptibly unguarded comments overheard or uttered over a period of weeks, plus of course the dejected look on the face of the sufferer looming across dining saloon and lounge.

More apparent were hints of a major row brewing in the engineers' domain, which came to us in the deck department via another set of occasional rumours and secretive glances between the juniors over coffee. I was playing chess as usual with the senior third engineer one evening when his mind was clearly not on the game. In fact, he played so appallingly that I thoroughly thrashed him and as we put away the pieces (literally and metaphorically) he opened up sufficiently to share more details. I listened, and offered a little encouragement by asking a couple of casual questions (filing away his remarks mentally for later dissemination between us mates). Of such nefarious substance is the nature of shipboard inter-departmental loyalty. As the next senior officer, Charles found himself acting as a buffer between the opposing factions of the chief, second and the junior engineers, even though in this respect his sympathies lay with the juniors. The dispute apparently revolved around the amount of dirty money offered as a bonus by the company for specifically unsocial jobs falling by definition to the lot of their department. He shut up then, realising he had said too much and already mindful that rivalry on the chessboard was inevitably also reflected across social areas. Anyway, it seemed the matter was being discussed between the chief and the company, while the juniors were contacting our mutual union, the Merchant Navy and Airline Officers' Association (MNAOA), seeking their intervention. I had joined them as a cadet, but valued my membership more once I became certificated. This was not so much to enjoy their fringe benefits of discounts at some stores ashore, but for the free insurance cover provided should any officer's certificate of competency be attacked in circumstances that needed defending by a barrister anywhere in the world. I had not been aware of their intervention in shipboard rows, never having had the need to invite them. Discussing the incident with Derek, Paul and Tim, admittedly with some non-malicious humour, we decided our sympathies also rested with the juniors. Eventually, the row was settled with the company paying the extra cash.

But wider cracks were appearing in the jovial bonhomie that had been so much a part of the crew's demeanour. Already, alcoholism had proved something of a problem with our deck crew, and the other two departments. The entire crowd had clearly purchased a considerable quantity of spirits from Las Palmas, although no officers reported seeing any cases coming on board. Certainly during some late evening watches I had received one or two bizarre phone calls from the bosun, which I attributed to him 'showing off' to his lads. I discussed this with Paul, who advised ignoring these incidents, but I took Bose quietly aside on the main deck one afternoon and told him point blank to stop doing this. He did not say anything but merely looked very sheepish and walked away: the phone calls, however, stopped! Paul did comment that Derek, the chief and Les had mentioned their lads showed signs of being well or slightly under the influence on various occasions. Mind you, I had noticed that Les appeared far more jovial and flush-faced as the day proceeded! I received an earful from another quarter each morning as the second steward brought a coffee tray into the wheelhouse for the master and me and increasingly started to make adverse comments regarding his other colleagues, especially Les, his immediate boss. I not only brushed these off and changed the subject as soon as I could, but I also started to pre-empt the opening pause upon his popping the tray onto the chart table. He proved to be a pretty thick-skinned character though and, among some other interesting habits, showed a definite interest in the younger catering boy! Such, it appeared, was a part of life with deep-sea European crews not experienced on the coast.

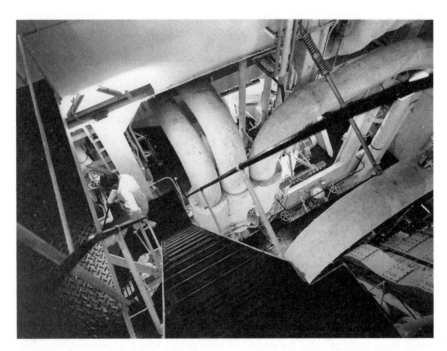

This rare shot of the entrance to the engine room indicated a venue rarely taken in by most deck officers, in the same way that few found their way to the wheelhouse. There was nothing particularly significant in this, for officers were invariably bounded strictly by duties: if you were not working in a particular venue then you rarely ventured there. (BP plc)

★ ★ ★

Running down the coast off the Columbine Light on the last leg before passing Cape Town, I saw ahead a collection of cargo ships almost in accidental convoy spread over perhaps 7 miles. With recent memories in mind, and a previous lesson learnt, I altered course wide to starboard, taking the entire 'fleet' down our port side. It was again appreciated how much the height of the radar scanner above sea level detected targets very early, giving ample time to deduce possible courses and distances (under normal circumstances) and so allowing for any necessary avoiding action to be taken almost imperceptibly by altering our course only a few degrees. Frequently, I was the only person on the ship aware that we had altered.

Exactly three weeks after leaving Helsingør we passed a few miles off Cape Town. I just had time for lunch after being relieved promptly by Paul before returning to the wheelhouse, standing by for meeting the launch, which came out to the vessel and adjusted its speed to meet our reduced engine revolutions. While the chief officer had already supervised raising our midships port-side derrick he subsequently stood by for taking on local stores, as well as a junior engineering officer who was replacing one whose alcohol intake exceeded that which the chief engineer considered acceptable. We also discharged our group of Finnish fitters who, completing their labour of love, had left us the proud possessors of a complete set of zinc anodes in all ballast tanks.

We passed 14 miles abeam Cape Agulhas at 1110 hrs during my watch next day, to take maximum advantage of a favourable Agulhas current. The master had left me to make the bold alteration to our course line from 129 degrees (T) to 068 degrees (True and Gyro) heading towards Cape Recife at Port Elizabeth on passage up the African coast, so consequently I was very surprised on hearing the chartroom door open to see him appear in the wheelhouse. Giving a very quizzical look, he asked why I had not altered course at the specified time and stated his thought that I 'may have been frozen to the spot'. In response, I did not say anything but merely directed his attention to the passing fully laden Esso

Taking on stores was invariably a routine task as most VLCCs passed off Cape Town. On our first voyage these were taken from a launch, and included seasonal foodstuffs as well as replacement books and films. Replacement personnel were also occasionally carried. *(Both BP plc)*

VLCC *Esso Indonesia* of around 261,230sdwt that was passing down our port side. He looked at the ship, smiled, and told me he had not noticed the low-laden tanker from his starboard-side accommodation window. He then gave that famous smile and said, 'It would have been very ironic if we had collided with a tanker not only from my old company, but one I have previously commanded!' My own smile was adequate response as we watched her pass down safely. When she was well clear of our beam I put the helm onto manual steering and conned our vessel onto her new course. I was surprised that he did not speak to her on our VHF radio system for he would almost certainly have known someone senior on board, but thought it prudent not to ask any questions. This incident proved to be significant because it acted as a 'breakthrough moment'. From that moment, while still retaining strict professionalism, we began building new levels of personal understanding.

Most of the ports up the West African coast held a veritable host of pleasant memories from my dry-cargo ship days. I had always been attracted by the names of some of these navigational landmarks while watching them pass down our port side: Duiker, Slangkop, Olifantisbos, and the obviously named Barracouta, with Struys and Yzervack appearing among the more exotic.

The Comoro Islands in the Mozambique Channel were taken down our port side at a safe distance. Bizarrely (or at least so it seemed to me), none of this group were lit so we had to rely on radar ranges and bearings to give them a wide berth. The senior catering boy was well advanced towards completing his statutory thirty hours steering instruction, so I called him to the wheelhouse and let him take the wheel for an extra session, so giving his tuition at least some sense of purpose.

We had just cleared the islands, the boy had gone below and I had put the gyro back onto automatic when our heading dropped off course. This was the first time since passing off the Dogger Bank it had happened, but I was so quick off the mark the poor old alarm did not have a chance to sound. I placed my look-out on the wheel, called the standby man, and notified the master. He called Sparks to the bridge and

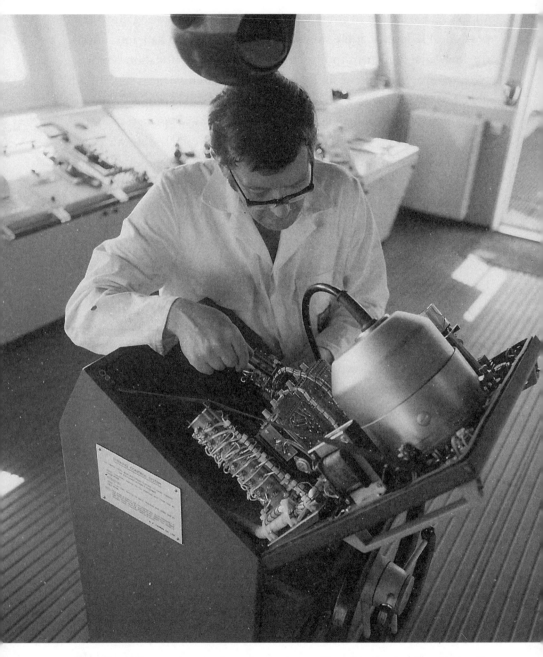

The Decca Arkas steering console rarely gave any problems, but occasionally some gremlin intervened caused sometimes by excessive vibration when these large ships were in ballast. (BP plc)

after a while 'tinkering about with the gubbins' (as Ben professionally described his antics), the relays, which had apparently burnt out, were replaced. What with a few mishaps with engine room gear, some of the deck equipment, and the galley there was, as Derek described the circumstances, 'never a dull moment aboard this hooker'. The incident that had put the galley range out of action meant our entire crew spent a day without hot meals, but we were more than compensated by an ingenious and quite filling array of salads and sandwiches that Les provided. I also had experienced problems with ship's gear during my first fire and boat drill for, of the first four hoses I tried, three were non-functional. Between all departments we certainly helped our guarantee chief engineer justify his existence!

★ ★ ★

On occasions when I was not working with the master on deck for two or three hours each afternoon, or continuing my tedious but necessary 'paint tapping' exercises, I spent a lot of time with Derek being shown the machinations and having explained the workings of the piping, pumping and cargo and ballast systems. We both knew that none of this would really 'click in' until I had completed my first and probably second sessions each of loading and discharging crude oil, but at least the knowledge imbibed, in the words of my esteemed captain, 'prepared the groundwork for better things'.

Bringing the vessel round to 017 degrees (T) heading *Rania Chandris* for the Arabian Gulf, the thought crossed my mind that it seemed odd to pass Socotra Island Light at right angles off the port side. Usually my trading cleared the thing to starboard, heading for Dondra Head, the southern tip of Sri Lanka, or altering to pop down the east African coast. The stretches of water up to and in Gulf waters were completely new to me and the first thing I noticed was how the temperature shot up after we passed a safe 30 miles abeam of Ras Yei Point on Masirah Island. A heavy mugginess affected all on board when out on the bridge wings

A forward tank bulkhead showing, under construction, line pipes, staggered ladder, and the anodes fitted into all ballast tanks to help combat corrosion. (Shell ITS)

or deck, away from our suddenly appreciated air-conditioned accommodation. This was not the only change experienced, for the abnormal atmospheric effects produced anomalous spurious echoes on the radar: a ship would be sighted dead ahead on the 12-mile range on equal and opposite speed to our own vessel, only to disappear after being followed down to 3 miles. The clue, of course, as I quickly discovered, was in the 'equal and opposite course and speed', although that did not preclude constant monitoring of the set in addition to keeping a visual lookout.

It was also shortly after clearing Ras al Hadd and setting a course 320 degrees (T) to clear Didamur Light, marking the entrance to the Arabian Gulf after passing through the Gulf of Oman, that details were received concerning our loading port and cargo. I came on watch next day to find the log book daily entry heading had been changed from 'Helsingør towards Persian Gulf for Orders (PGFO)' to the oil terminal attached to Kharg Island at the north-eastern part of the Gulf, roughly 16 miles off Bushire. We were to load a full cargo of crude oil for an unspecified port in Europe. After coming from dry-cargo ships where cargo was loaded for very specific destinations, this apparent anomaly 'of a ship not knowing where she was going' seemed vaguely humorous but realistically unique to the tanker trades. It was something else to which I had to become accustomed but the reason became more understandable when I learnt that tankers often loaded around one month ahead of discharging, leaving pundits in the office ashore scouting around for the best deal on what could, after all, be 286,000 tons of crude. This, without too much exaggeration and placed in better practically understandable terms, could theoretically, depending on temperature and specific gravity of the oil, be as much as 84 million gallons. This phenomenal quantity was breathtaking. My mind had finally run out of superlatives concerning this ship and everything associated with her! Captain Agnew told me later that this brand new vessel was paid for after just a few voyages and that subsequently, less the operating costs of which fuel oil and total crew wages were bulk items, *Rania Chandris* ran at a profit for her owners.

A typical photo of the third officer at work plotting the ship's position surrounded by the main computerised anti-collision radar, depth sounder, chronometer in its case, and associated navigating instruments. (BP plc)

It was from this point that severe vibration set into the ship. This was explained as being caused by commencing discharge of some ballast water in preparation for loading. It affected all areas of the ship but was particularly noticeable in the wheelhouse, where our handwriting in the log book looked as if all officers were suffering a particularly difficult form of ague. Even worse was the potential for errors to be introduced into our sextants, but understanding engineers, expressing some interest in having the ship arrive somewhere near her destination, happily provided us with beds of thick sorbo-type material upon which to place our trusty guns in case the impossible should happen.

For some days, Paul's ears had been assailed from nearly all of our 'tanker types' from master to crew enquiring, 'When do we pass the Quoins?' leaving me all agog to see this landmark for myself. It was 0815 so I enjoyed passing the three roughly wedge-shaped islands appearing slap bang central in the main channels that gave this important transit point to and from the Gulf its colloquial nickname. Captain Agnew was already on the bridge after I relieved Tim and he gave me a direct glance as I came out to the steering binnacle where my quartermaster had just relieved the helm. He smiled at my barely hidden interest in these 'weird sisters' (as I quoted *Macbeth*) but did not comment on the literary associations with my allusion.

I had three distinct impressions. My first was the number of laden tankers representing the whole range of crude oil tonnage coming towards us out of the heavy heat haze. There was an unbroken convoy with one ship passing us every few minutes as regularly as trains running into Waterloo. Luckily, as the master explained in uncharacteristically lurid terms, compulsory adherence to the traffic separation zones imposed order out of the absolute chaos existing before these were introduced. I also noticed that adherence to regulations did not extend universally across all maritime areas. The gibberish chatter, bird calls and extreme language emanating from distress channel 16 on our VHF radio was vaguely disturbing. Captain Agnew called these utterances 'severe attacks of tankeritis', restricted (luckily) to some who had served tankers for too long a period without leave. My final impression was felt rather than observed as an even greater increase in heat hit me when I went onto the bridge wings to take visual bearings. The time of the year we had hit the Gulf coincided with the monsoon season, and I certainly noticed it.

Strange things happened to most of our navigating gear, which caused Sparks no end of problems and left him and Paul cursing as they dismantled the gyro compass that had celebrated entering the Gulf by producing a series of course slips. The auxiliary radar blacked out by failing to produce any sort of picture, the direction finder suddenly offered a range of bizarrely inaccurate readings, and the Decca Navigator failed to come in well, with the relevant wheels whirling around at speeds consistent with the ship's propeller. These things continued throughout the first day, with the helm placed onto manual steering and a deck boy gaining some excellent tuition under the supervision of Geordie. I made a note in my personal records that: 'the gear these last couple of days has been a real ★★★!'

Above and opposite: *Servicing the radar and master gyro compass were generally routine duties, although the former often required more elaborate attention, arising from dirty contacts more than anything of a sinister nature. (Both BP plc)*

I had worked daily with Paul since leaving Denmark, taking noon sights and assisting with his chart corrections, and this had given added interest to my own bridge work. He had always been both supportive and very helpful and, as he relieved me while on passage between the Quoins and Kharg Island, he mentioned that Captain Agnew had stated his future intentions of recommending my promotion to second officer after Paul had left the ship to take his first mates' certificate upon completion of our current tour of voyages. Probably with this in mind, Captain Agnew sent me aft with Paul, as he stated, 'to observe him taking the vessel alongside and preparing you to act as second officer later when, of course, you will be expected to do this'. This was the first time he had actually stated his intentions. I felt progress was being made.

★ ★ ★

Coming alongside starboard side to proved an interesting operation, to put things mildly. While Paul looked after the preparation of our moorings, he gave me a deckhand and left me to take wires from a total of three tugs after pointing out the various bollards spread forward of the accommodation and down the port side and off the starboard quarter, to which the pilot wanted them made fast. Apart from the unusual number (for most dry-cargo ships rarely took on more than one tug aft) the only other difference noticed was the merciless sun blazing from a cloudless sky, with temperatures exceeding 110°F in an excessively dry heat. Luckily, the unaccustomed hard hat issued to all deck officers was made of very light but strong material and a sweat rag around the internal rim helped make this a more comfortable item to wear. The process of coming alongside was lengthy, although interesting to observe, prolonged by the linesmen being in dispute with their management regarding overtime and pay differentials and consequently operating a 'go slow'. The pilot explained these circumstances to the master, who lost no time passing on this little love message to his officers fore and aft. Not that we needed telling. I went aft at 0820 hrs after escorting the two pilots to the wheelhouse and handing them over to the master. We stood down with the vessel finally in position alongside at 1325, giving us all a stand-by lasting five hours, something to the order of three hours over an average time for a VLCC to come alongside a jetty, and over four hours longer than berthing one of my cargo vessels.

Once we were in position alongside, Bose and the ABs set up fire wires, one each fore and aft, making the vessel ready for tugs to tow us off the berth in the event of any serious emergency, and the duty QM also attended the moorings and gangway, adjusting these as the tanker settled more deeply into the water as loading progressed. Geordie worked conscientiously and well for all cargo watches, proving how totally reliable he could be, when he chose …

Popping into the saloon for lunch, I noticed a distinct chilling in the atmosphere that had little to do with the air conditioning. I noticed

Tim was not present at his table place between Derek and Paul but, with the former busily engaged on deck duties, had assumed he was busy elsewhere. It seemed he was, but not in the way I thought. The second hint of anything amiss was a pointed sideways look from Paul, which I immediately and correctly interpreted as 'keep quiet and I'll explain afterwards'. I had a pretty shrewd idea of the problem. When I had relieved Tim on the bridge occasional thoughts crossed my mind regarding his sobriety, and chatting with Paul, we wondered if alcoholism was the true reason why Tim had left Mobil. Anyway, after we had finished coffee in the saloon and in the privacy of his cabin, Paul explained that both the master and pilot had problems communicating with Tim on the fo'c'sle and were becoming exasperated by the slow rate that tugs were being taken and moorings put out, notwithstanding the shore labour dispute. Eventually, Derek had been despatched from what were my duties in the wheelhouse and sent for'rard to relieve Tim from the mooring operation. He had seemingly taken to his cabin after this and had not reappeared.

I remained off duty after lunch while the vessel completed discharging ballast. We retained our usual sea watches, unlike dry-cargo ships when deck officers usually went onto twelve-hour cargo shifts, so I started my first cargo operation at the usual relief time of 2000 hrs until midnight. As it happened, we did not commence loading until 2215, taking a full cargo in all tanks at an approximate rate averaging and building up to 10,000 tons per hour on each cargo pump.

The chief officer helped establish my routines. After opening the spark arresters fitted to all of the high-velocity ventilation valves, so allowing air to escape from the tanks as the crude gushed in under pressure from the four cargo pumps, I spent the entire watch visiting each wing and centre tank in turn recording cargo ullages, temperatures, and then taking draft readings. It was here that the capacity plan handed to me by Derek light years before in Helsingør came into its own. The mechanical gauges that measured ullages were producing highly inaccurate readings in some tanks, so Derek got the bosun to rig an excessively awkward hand line that reached 95ft to the bottom of the tank. This was weighted down by a large wooden wedge. The error for correction often varied as much as 3 to 4in. Lugging all of this paraphernalia along the best part of a quarter of a mile of main deck was no joke in the Gulf's heat, often well over 110°F during the night with day readings exceeding 120°F. As a new boy to tanker trading, I found it necessary to take a multitude of salt tablets every day, so replacing excessive body loss of fluids through good old-fashioned perspiration. Universally, we blessed the air-conditioning fitted in our accommodation, which enabled us all to relax in the dining room and lounge, and even more importantly enjoy a solid night's sleep.

Derek had started loading our single-grade crude oil cargo by filling the seventeen tanks gradually in series. This enabled our 286,000 tons of cargo to be completed at different rates, with average ullages around 5ft 9in and prevented an otherwise suddenly hectic flurry of rushing around the decks. Thus, loading was carried out at a leisurely and efficient completion, over approximately twenty-nine hours. He explained this was a good rate of loading and had occurred without too many stoppages and delays, which all too frequently bedevilled any kind of tanker cargo operation. This statement was not necessary to amplify and neither did I need to ask, for I had already appreciated for many years that, typical of all Merchant Naval procedures, things rarely went according to best-laid plans.

I felt decidedly alone as Derek went to 'get his head down', having left instructions for me or whoever happened to be on duty to call him when the first ullage in the port slop tank aft read his desired 5ft 9in. But my mind was soon occupied as I became very busy taking ullages and temperatures across all centre tanks and keeping an eye on the draft of the vessel. Bose had assigned a deck boy to Geordie for training, so I left them happily tending our moorings sandwiched between keeping an eye on the gangway for visitors. Certainly my confidence increased by opening and closing appropriate valves as I had been previously taught, while dealing with cargo watch actions upon which I had never previously focused.

The deck seemed to have an almost ethereal atmosphere in the warm sticky evening. Unshielded lights glared from our own lamp posts and jetty, casting lengthy shadows between the mazes of piping once seemingly so complicated, but now becoming increasingly familiar as I learnt where each one went and understood more of its function. The four-hour watch seemed to go well as I busily entered my readings into our record book, and could not believe how soon Paul appeared. Shooting me his usual friendly grin, he tapped my shoulder, and took over the watch and record of loading. Walking towards the accommodation block, I experienced a sense of relief: the tanker still stood upright, showing no signs of sinking or capsizing, but it was still delightfully pleasant entering our cool accommodation and taking the lift to the navigating officers' deck. A quick shower followed by my traditional maritime pre-sleeping read soon led into a settled and deep sleep.

Just before noon I went out on deck to relieve Tim, only to find Derek up by number two centre tank taking ullages and temperatures. He glanced up as he explained cargo progress and then, with his inimitably quiet smile, told me that Tim was not only incapable, but had caused a slight oil spill earlier in his watch that had stopped cargo for an hour while the crew rallied round clearing up the mess. The delay had aroused questions ashore and their cargo inspector had appeared on our ship seeking further information regarding reasons for the delay. Luckily, the spillage was not too severe and none had gone over the side into the harbour. If this had occurred, Derek explained, the ship would have been subjected to a massive fine.

On the next cargo watch, I was staggered to find Paul still on watch. Fuming, he explained Tim had failed to relieve him so, being far too busy to leave the deck duties, he had been forced into an extra four-hour stint on deck. He had sent his AB to knock on Tim's cabin door, but the man had returned to say he was unable to gain any response.

For the rest of us, life went on comparatively normally: we just got on with our own duties and built these around Tim's continued absences.

It was interesting to conclude my next cargo watch with Derek, participating as directed in the final stages of loading called 'topping off'.

We completed cargo at 0450 the following day, having taken a full load of the same-grade Iranian crude and leaving port with a mean draft of 74ft 11in.

Tim continued in a 'bad way', to coin an expression. As Derek was still snowed under with essential duties associated with a new build and was forced to remain on day work, Captain Agnew told Paul and me that it was best to rearrange our watches. This would be at least 'for a couple of days until Tim could be relied upon to carry out watch-keeping duties'. It came over to us both quite clearly from the determined look in the master's eyes that if Tim could not sort himself out quickly then he would be relieved at Cape Town, flown home and dismissed from the company. However reassuring that might have sounded, Paul was quick to point out that Cape Town was something like fifteen days away.

As I was now on watch from 0600 hrs, the master left me to snooze happily in my cosy bunk until a seven-bell call at 0530. As Derek arrived to give me a meal relief for thirty or forty minutes he encouraged me with a wide grin, saying ambiguously, 'Ray, I am sorry about the extra two hours on each watch for you and Paul, but you are undoubtedly well on the way to becoming a real tanker man.'

★ ★ ★

Tanker man or not was still highly debatable in my opinion, but on watch as we crossed the Gulf heading for the Quoins it was time to take stock and consolidate what, as a dedicated 10,000-ton dry-cargo ship man, I had imbibed. While going in the opposite capacity direction and listening to the other mates talking professionally about loading our cargo and using loosely bandied-around terms, now that I had helped load my first oil cargo, the whole operation took on some deeper significance. It had quickly become apparent that there were two types of cargo measurement. For when they spoke about quantities in terms of barrels rather than tons, I knew now they were referring to oil in terms of its volume, and when tons were mentioned I was aware this was a measurement of oil quantity in terms of weight. It was staggering to find we had taken on something just below 300,000 barrels. 'Ullage' was the term used that, to coin an expression for learners, denoted the amount of oil that was not in the tank (!), representing the space between the top of the oil and the underside of the tank. Temperature, in the knowledge of school physics lessons, was the only one that remained pretty obvious. But at least I was beginning to make the necessary connections between these important measurements and so understand more about what I was doing when these were taken.

I glanced anew at the familiar table called the Merchant Shipping (Load Line) Rules displayed in the chartroom, which gave a still operative 1968 list of zones, areas and seasonal periods. This divided the world into a series of regions related to the readily recognisable and familiar load line that we carried on each of the midships sides of our tanker. Now relating the connection between the two started to make a different, more significant, type of sense. To make passage to Europe, we had to leave the Tropical Zone from where we loaded, and cross the Summer Zone, until we reached Cape Torifiana in Spain and, proceeding north, entered the appropriate seasonal North Atlantic zone. The oil expands and contracts, hence the reason for not loading to 100 per cent capacity because, as we crossed the zone boundaries, our cargo cooled in the different temperatures of sea water encountered and decreased in volume. Thus, had we loaded at a temperature of 100°F, should the cargo cool to say 80°F then we would be transporting fewer barrels.

It was with a continuing but (my friends may have said) unaccustomed humility that I realised how much more there was to learn.

CHAPTER FOUR

CONTINUING THE LEARNING CURVE

As if to celebrate our departure from the Gulf, the bridge gear played up unmercifully! Our pride and joy, the main radar, packed up completely, leaving me gazing at an unhelpfully blank screen and having to rely purely on the secondary set. 'Mr Solly, it is like driving a mini after a Rolls-Royce,' was the Old Man's accurate description of the situation. He made no further comment after learning that the gyro had slipped on three occasions during my watch, and the secondary radar also packed up once while changing from a 12-mile range for a 'look-see' to observe what was happening ahead of the vessel, to a normal working range of 6 miles. From 1030 hours, readings on the Decca Navigator were unreliable. I was not sure about the Direction Finder as, rightly or wrongly, I tried obtaining readings from this, but these were also totally unreliable. They gave a suggested fix placing the ship somewhere in the Indian Ocean, so I switched it off. Poor old Ben was again not a happy electronics bunny as he came directly from keeping his two-hourly radio watch to give what at first was tender loving care, although even his patience wore thin as he admitted being unable to sort out the muddle we had prepared for him 'to stop you getting bored', as I put it, taking his black look with due aplomb! The only other thing of any note was observing, and taking avoiding collision action for, three tankers contravening the traffic separation rules and heading directly for us. Geordie, with an acceptable sense of humour for once, declared, 'Third, I wonder if they have heard that our menu is an improvement on theirs.'

In between twice-daily sights, it was interesting to take the ship off automatic and steer her manually when rounding headlands and altering course for anti-collision purposes. She was certainly far more sluggish on the helm than when in ballast but, once she started to alter, her momentum brought her round very quickly so that an almost immediate counter-helm had to be applied. My continued work with Paul covered a range of duties including those not only with the numerous chart corrections, but also sorting out corrections and amendments to a host of associated maritime publications covering the world. We filed away those in the Black, Barents and more obscure seas we would never use, but selected carefully from among others where supertankers might be called to serve.

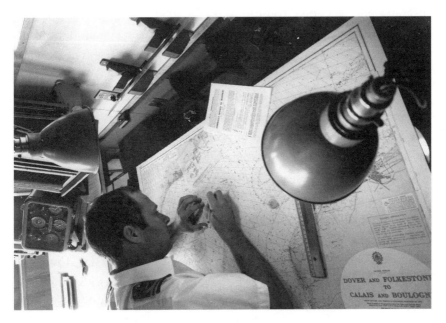

Chart corrections were a perennial task undertaken by the second officer, but often the third mate assisted as much to help a colleague as to gain experience for his next step up the promotion ladder. (BP plc)

My deck duties covered a range of interesting and instructive duties, ranging from a simple changing of a washer on the galley main water supply tap to working with the master and Danish chief engineer repairing a ballast suction pump in the lower reaches of the pump room. On another occasion, I joined Captain Agnew in dropping through the rat hole in the bosun's store and inspecting the fore peak water ballast tank. It was a strange experience being at the most forward and lowest parts of the ship scrambling over the deck construction parts. And quite awesome listening to the thud of seas forced apart by the powerful thrust of our 23,000shp engine and feeling underfoot and ahead a more unaccustomed motion now associated with this ship.

It was with more than a sigh of relief that I completed my paint assessments on all parts of the main deck and machinery where the stuff had been applied. I had found no discrepancies with the specifications in the maker's manual but, as Derek explained somewhat laconically as I dropped my paint measurer onto his desk: 'You had to do the job in order to find that out!' I could think of no slick answer to this sage comment. As our deck hands busily touched up paintwork on deck that already showed signs of assault by the salt-laden air and actually being trodden on, another task was checking the remaining deck stores of oil, paints and other nautical sundries to help him prepare indent forms for sending by radio to our next port.

Cargo deck work included checking temperatures and ullages and measuring these against the latter readings on the measurement gauges with our handy drop gear of rope and wedge. My two open lifeboats required regular maintenance. This including changing cases of condensed milk tins and fresh water once per trip, as well as keeping an eye on the condition of paint and varnish work, although at this early stage of the ship's life these showed little sign of weathering. By now I was well familiar with the placing of gear associated with my other LSA duties, so I checked lifebuoys, life rafts, safety lamps and fire extinguishers regularly. I had also taken a note of all serial numbers, knowing from dry-cargo ship days that these would be required at some stage for Lloyd's Registry and other inspections of equipment, to which all ships are subjected.

Open lifeboats on the older VLCCs created their own set of problems for the third officer, under whose responsibility their maintenance rested. Much scraping of paintwork and revarnishing was needed to keep them in good condition. (Ray Solly)

It took Tim two days before he was able to resume his bridge and deck work, but this proved more of a lull than permanent promise. Just four days later passing off Mogadiscio (now Mogadishu) found me relieving Paul once more. A deeply penitent Tim made his guest star appearance two days later off Beira, but this venture was also doomed to failure as by the time we passed Durban he was out of action once more. During his more sober moments, Tim was deeply penitent, explaining to all, sundry and anyone else who had the patience to listen that his total dependence upon alcohol had already ruined his career with Mobil – and his marriage. He expressed, and we believed him, he was at his wits' end to find a way out. The only suggestions we could make were to suggest he continued seeking help from Alcoholic Anonymous through the medical profession. I felt sorry for him, but knew from my own maritime experience observing all too many others that once 'demon drink' took hold of a person it was the devil's own job to break this particular mould. In the meantime, life went on, with Paul and me covering his eight-hour bridge watches.

Other routine maintenance on lifeboats included cleaning emergency lighting, and replacing water and condensed milk included among emergency rations. (BP plc)

One interesting and different drill performed by the entire deck department after one of our weekly lifeboat lowering and raising exercises on Saturday afternoons at 1600 hrs was to rescue Fred from the bottom of a ballast tank. Fred was a life-sized and realistically weighted dummy that Derek had arranged with two of the three QMs to be placed in the most inaccessible part of the tank. The supervision of this operation was left to me, and it proved a formidable task. Derek had warned me beforehand, exerting his brand of somewhat wry humour, that he had set up a treat for me when my party was next on the stretcher drill. The first I knew the drill had started was when Geordie (who had not participated in the preparations), grinning all over his face, came and reported there had been an accident to a crew member in the starboard ballast tank forming the after part of number two wings. I sent him and two of my crew to the Butterworth locker midships to collect the portable lifting gear, telling them to take it to the tank top. I also sent an AB with the deck boys to bring the Neilson stretcher. I knew we would be working in very close confines and that too many men would have got in the way of each other so, taking just Geordie and three experienced crew members, I descended to the tank bottom to find Fred. Then, the fun began. His literal deadweight had to be strapped into the stretcher and manoeuvred through a system of man and rat holes until he was in a more accessible part of the tank below the tank inspection hatch. While the lads on deck, especially the deck boys, treated the task with some hilarity, I supervised my group with a more measured air of relaxed authority. My mind was preoccupied with the 'what if' reality of this potential situation, as if Fred had been a real person.

European crew generally aboard this hooker had been 'something of a pain' compared to my Asian crews (to put things mildly) but faced with an emergency or a serious task they responded with supportive responsibility. In fact, the lads were superb. Once they had sweated Fred into position with the stretcher secured to the lowered line with a suitable bowline, both were raised to the main deck. I carefully checked the bowline following an accident to a stevedore when I served on a

Rescuing a dummy from the bottom
of a tank was an emergency drill often
undertaken aboard tankers. This was a
difficult task that was usually supervised
by the third officer, and necessitated
manoeuvring, with associated contortions, a
life-sized and weight straw figure through
manholes and rat holes before hoisting him
to the main deck. (All three Shell ITS)

dry-cargo ship in Santiago de Cuba. The other dock workers, instead of waiting for the second officer to arrive (who happened to be myself!) and supervise sorting out the accident, had gone ahead anyway. They tied some sort of knotted abortion, which sadly started giving way when stretcher and patient were some 20ft above the hold bottom. I had shouted to the Spanish-speaking winchman to lower immediately, but owing to language problems he had not reacted sufficiently quickly, so the stretcher plummeted some 15ft to the bottom of the hold. I can hear still the sickening crash as this tragic load hit the hard sacks of cargo. The appalling sound will doubtless remain for the rest of my life. As an even more disgusting finale, the port authorities left the man by the gangway covered by a tarpaulin, seeping a runnel of blood into the scuppers for five hours before the mortuary van arrived to collect him. So far as our efforts were concerned, with Fred laid to rest in the bosun's stores, Derek, who had timed the complete mock operation, expressed his satisfaction with our combined efforts. 'You now have this job for life, especially if we need it for real,' was his laconic comment to me. 'Ah, gee, thanks,' was my own equally terse response.

★ ★ ★

It had to be during my watch as *Rania Chandris* approached Cape Recife some 20 miles off Port Elizabeth that we ran into storm-force 10, gusting 12, winds (which was at the maximum of Beaufort's famous scale). Such storms were not common but were associated with the prevalent south-west monsoons. It had already been blowing force 7 when I relieved Paul and within a couple of hours the full extent of a 'southern African beauty', as he termed this, took full effect. I had already agreed with the duty engineer he should reduce revolutions to a speed of 7 knots before Captain Agnew appeared in the wheelhouse. He promptly told me to take off a further 3 knots. This eased the motion considerably, reducing pounding damage to the bows and fore part of the ship, but did little to ease the 35 degrees overall roll to which the ship was subjected. I was

Tankers voyaging through seas and winds of often storm force or even higher were prone to considerable hull stresses and strains invariably requiring an easing of engines. These extremes of weather could appear suddenly in any ocean or seas in the world. (Both Ray Solly)

quite surprised that a vessel of our size would react so comparatively violently to these admitted extremes of weather, although the motion was modest compared with the violent swinging of my dry-cargo ships, where the inclinometer often swung to extremes exceeding an over-all 90 degrees. This latter motion on both classes of ship was invariably accompanied by severe pitching and rolling, although extremes on the VLCC in these other directions were more modest in comparison.

Needless to say, the bridge gear continued playing up. The main radar remained totally dead, while the picture on our secondary kept fading as we changed downwards the ranges. The gyro slipped at least once or twice every hour, knocking the ship up to 10 degrees off course. I got so fed up with adjusting the thing that I called Geordie away from his deck work, knocked the steering off automatic and set him handling the vessel manually. Eventually, I arranged with Derek and the bosun for the deck boys to take a trick each during daytime for some serious steering practice, releasing the more experienced QMs for other duties. The secondary radar then gave up the ghost shortly after we cleared the Mozambique Channel. It was just after 0900 as we passed Cape Recife that the third engineer phoned to say that they were experiencing alternator problems and needed to reduce speed even further. Ten minutes later we had a complete electrical blackout and the vessel slowed delicately to a stop. As the deck boy was now superfluous to requirements I set him the task of drawing the Not Under Command (NUC) shapes from the after bridge locker and showed him how to bend these onto the signal halyard, leaving him to raise them above the monkey island. I then retained him for lookout duties. On this occasion we were drifting for eight hours.

Captain Agnew often popped on and off the bridge, sorting out paperwork and invariably stopping for a casual chat. The more dealings I had with this man, the more I respected him. I had invariably formed a firmly relaxed professional relationship with most of the masters under whose command I had sailed, but there seemed to be developing something deeper with him. We just seemed to click. He never swore or used bad language at all, which was quite unprecedented for any mariner, but when something ruffled his feathers he would merely say 'Oh my goodness, Mr Solly ...' and then comment on whatever had roused his ire. I first noticed this after departure from Las Palmas when my morning watch was entertained as he and the mate logged many of the once-again sober crew. He had just a few guarded words to say to the crew individually as they were each fined one day's pay, but I overheard far deeper comments being exchanged with Derek regarding this incident, hinting vaguely about his report to the company and even more vaguely suggesting perhaps a way forward. About the delayed mooring incident in Kharg Island, and regarding Tim, he said nothing in my presence.

There was invariably a mass of administrative paperwork associated with the running of his ship to keep most ship's masters busy. Tasks included keeping a record of events in the official log-book, voyage letters to the directors and running the ship's portage bill. (BP plc)

Fifteen days out of Kharg Island we passed off Cape Town. The port authorities advised that we would now and on all subsequent voyages be served by a duty helicopter that had finally replaced the traditional launch. We were given a VHF channel to make and maintain contact with the pilot, and it was not long before he was hovering over the speci- fied area on our main deck. I was on watch in the wheelhouse and it was fascinating to follow the echo of the copter racing across the screen on our secondary set. Derek was in charge of the entire operation, supervis- ing the bosun and deck crew to use our trolley and take on an assortment of catering, deck and engine room stores, a film and library exchange and very welcome mail. We also took replacement parts both for our gyrocompass and Decca Arkas steering gear. Quick farewells were said to a very subdued Tim, who was returning to the UK and an uncertain maritime future, but an electronics engineer from a radar consortium based in the Cape was taken on board to sort out our two sets. As he was unleashed from the lowering gear, Paul and I mistook him initially for our replacement first officer. We were soon disillusioned. Captain Agnew explained who the person was and told us the company had been unable to find a replacement for Tim. We both looked askance, realising that covering his bridge watches would have to continue for a further twelve days until Las Palmas when, we were promised, another officer would definitely be flown to the ship.

Ben and the specialist engineer quickly unpacked their boxes of 'radar goodies' and got to work. There was some urgency, as the man would not be travelling with us but 'as soon as he had completed his work would be uplifted by the helicopter again', as Captain Agnew expressed this. We also hoped that we too would be uplifted after the combined ministra- tions by having two radar sets that actually worked.

Taking over the remainder of my watch, I was the first navigator to alter our entry in the log book from 'Kharg Island towards Land's End for Orders' (which had immediately been abbreviated to LEFO) to now read 'towards Lyme Bay'. This was a popular ship-to-ship transfer lightering point where we would offload some of our cargo into a smaller tanker.

Replacement of the launch delivering stores, personnel and film and book libraries off Cape Town by a helicopter proved of immeasurable benefit to the ship, as she no longer had to come off charter for a while by reducing speed. (BP plc)

This operation facilitated our deep-draught vessel to proceed up the English Channel towards Europoort, and onwards to the deep-water VLCC jetty at Coryton in the River Thames. I was still on watch when we offloaded our shore engineer back into his helicopter, although the operation on deck was again supervised by Derek.

In the way of the tanker world, three days later our orders were changed. We were now to proceed towards Finnart in Scotland, hence to Milford Haven, where we would complete discharge. It was with great relief that we found ourselves proud possessors of two radars and a steering gear that worked efficiently and reliably. The deck boys, to their chagrin we suspected, were returned to their normal more menial deck duties and I saw Geordie only when he cleaned the wheelhouse, external bridge areas and brass work, and for lookout duties during hours of darkness. Although Paul and I again covered six-hour watches, the QMs retained their normal four-hour watches so, in the overlap, it was interesting to share some of these periods with Paul's duty man. He was an elderly seafarer of many years' experience, quiet in demeanour and personality. He showed me three of his old discharge books, which were falling apart from usage and basically good old-fashioned old age. Out of respect, I took my time repairing these to make a good job and was quietly rewarded by his looks of appreciation as these clearly valued records were received back. Luke was a real 'shell back', as the expression goes. He had never worked ashore, had served through the entire Second World War on BP and Shell tankers with, I suspected, more than his fair share of incidents, although his natural reticence (sadly) extended to cover this period, and he had never been on shore leave for more than six months in his entire working life. Two of these periods had been survivors' leave. Captain Agnew saw me hard at work on the books and, glancing through them, commented on the value of such a man.

A helicopter flew a replacement officer for Tim as we passed Las Palmas. Douglas Lacey was in his late 50s, had gained his masters' certificate some thirty years earlier and had served on dry-cargo ships in all ranks up to chief officer. He came with a strong recommendation from

The chief officer worked the bosun and his deck crew on the almost permanent tasks of keeping the main deck clean and presentable. Obviously as the main walk way along the vessel, this received considerable punishment, not only from normal wear and tear but also contributions made by the weather. (Both BP plc)

London office as 'having tanker experience' but this proved to be aboard two product tankers of around 20,000sdwt fifteen years previously. Still, as Derek remarked with typically laconic smile and as positive as ever, 'Even this knowledge could prove useful.'

★ ★ ★

The ship had just cleared South Rock Light and we were 8 miles south of Ailsa Craig. I had changed to BA Chart 2724, settling her onto a new course line of 013 degrees True and Gyro, when Captain Agnew came into the wheelhouse. Glancing at him casually, I thought he looked a little preoccupied. Anyway, I carried on contemplating the bizarre antics of yet another fishing boat as it approached increasingly closely off our port bow, trying to determine just what the hell was going on in her wheelhouse. Just as I reached for the Aldis, drawing her attention to the international signal indicating our restricted ability to manoeuvre in confined waters due to the supertanker's obviously loaded condition, the thing suddenly altered course and shot off further to starboard. Replacing the lamp and sharing an understanding smile with the master, he came over to the front of the wheelhouse and, in quite sombre tones, asked me if I would be happy to be relieved from my watch and subsequent berthing duties at Finnart to pop into his study and help him sort out his portage bill. This apparently 'was in a bit of a mess and needed a fresh approach'.

I was actually familiar with this little fellow (to use a distinct euphemism) as I had helped a captain with his while serving as third officer on a previous deep-sea, dry-cargo ship. It was universally accepted among masters as 'a sod of a job', being a full voyage record of all financial transactions affecting every rating on the ship. Officers were paid directly into their bank accounts, so were not included. The bill covered such gems as items purchased from the slop chest (or ship's shop), pay, overtime, extra money for anything else, plus statutory deductions of income tax, national insurance, and allotment of money home: 'you name it and if it were financial, it appeared'. Just an unexpected extra day on the voyage could throw out all calculations. This necessitated many night hours trying to get the thing to balance vertically and horizontally before presenting it to the shipping master immediately upon arrival and paying off the crew.

So, after lunch and willingly forgoing any given opportunity of taking an afternoon zizz, I popped next door to the Old Man's study, listened as he explained his progress to date and then sat down with a calculator and, surrounded by various tables, prepared to offer his 'fresh approach'. I glanced through the bill, gaining an overall view of 'what was what', and then all of the supporting papers and tables. My task was restricted largely to checking Captain Agnew's figures, searching diligently (like one of the three biblical wise men) for the missing hypothetical sixpence that had literally created an imbalance – and mayhem. As I warmed to the task, becoming appropriately more focused, it was with much joy and rejoicing that I discovered a figure six that had clearly been mistaken for a zero. My popping into the wheelhouse coincided with the vessel in position alongside and the final line being made fast. The master's smile was just reward, so we were both 'happy nautical bunnies' as we joined the other officers at supper.

With a sigh of relief, my brief sojourn into the purser's department ended at 2000 hrs when I went on deck to relieve Douggie. He had proved a friendly enough guy who was unashamedly working towards retirement and declared he had even asked to be sent to the ship as second officer. I took to him instinctively, quickly adapting to his reliability and slow thinking. As Derek (it had to be) remarked, 'at least Douggie was always sober', being content merely to join the rest of us in an occasional glass of 'something according to taste' while relaxing off duty in the lounge, although the 'at least' spoke its own volumes.

I spent my watch continuing the task commenced by Douggie of opening the tank vents serving all port and starboard wing tanks, including working controls in the square boxes to open suction valves, and then standing by to begin the usual run of taking ullages once cargo

A square box containing hydraulic cargo valve controls serving numbers three, four and five centre tanks and wing tank fillings on the port side of the vessel. A total of thirty-nine valves controlled the oil flow in ten boxes. (Ray Solly)

Inside the same cargo deck control valves, showing cross-over lines between the tanks. (Ray Solly)

commenced at 2130. We were to discharge 70,000 tons of oil from the wing tanks in this BP port, afterwards proceeding to Angle Bay, where the centre and slops tanks would be emptied. It was a pretty straightforward operation and by the time Paul relieved me at midnight we had lowered our tanks by an average each of 2ft. Cargo was completed 0630 next day, coinciding with my breakfast call and enabling me to proceed to the wheelhouse for departure to Finnart half an hour later.

Seven miles slightly north-by-east of Ailsa Craig at 1130 hrs gave me one of those rare incidents that prove 'vignette' moments, ones of no importance whatsoever, but highly significant because they become permanently ingrained into the memory bank. I was returning to the wheelhouse having taken a final bearing of Plaida Isle Light when I focused on a previously noticed chap aboard a rowing boat fishing with rod and line. He suddenly seemed a far distant, minute figure to whom we must have appeared colossal. I know how I would have felt watching this monster of a ship just one mile away from my own diminutive craft steaming sedately past me. Looking in his direction, I gave him a brief wave that, to my surprise, he returned. But our exchange was more than a mere physical acknowledgement. The mutual gesture conveyed something of mutual affinity, a meeting of thoughts and emotions. I am convinced the guy also would remember our totally anonymous 'meeting'.

By the time I popped into the saloon next day, we were safely along-side the BP Ocean Terminal Berth 3. Captain Agnew and I were the only representatives of the deck department at breakfast as the others were either turned in or had gone ashore. He explained that unusually, even in his experience, the port authorities had advised they wanted to work our cargo through as one operation and, rather than having us anchor until they were ready, had taken us alongside until their tank capacity fell sufficiently. This meant we would not work cargo until the evening of the next day at the earliest. Derek had left me instructions in the cargo office of the work he wanted our crew to do, which I was to talk through with the bosun at 0800 hrs, along with some duties for Paul and me that would last us until 1600, when Derek would once more be out of deck.

The Chiksan connection at the main cargo manifolds midships served as connections between ship and shore. There were four main cargo lines plus extra lines for diesel oil and vapour return. (Ray Solly)

I set Bose accordingly on some deck painting and derrick work, telling him I wanted Geordie and Luke to work with me using secateurs and a compass to make four spare gaskets for the cargo manifold pipes. I also accompanied the port authorities closing sea chest valves, and testing cargo valves as necessary. Although they had completed the gaskets and returned on deck, I again grabbed my two ABs from Bose and used them to help me refit and tighten flanges on the starboard-side gas freeing fan, which had developed a minor leak. The remainder of this busy morning watch was spent taking and organising the crew along with the long-suffering bosun to load ship's stores for all departments and, inevitably, undertake my duties normally associated with deck watches alongside on board any ship. These included liaising with the duty engineer and keeping a general eye on the crew, particularly their smoke-oh and lunch periods, making sure (although with a certain latitude) these were not too much over-extended.

Flanges were fitted between the Chiksans and cargo pipes to make the fitting oil tight. A number of reduction pieces were used where necessary to cover differences in pipe circumferences. (Ray Solly)

After serving as duty officer overnight, I was told by Derek over breakfast the rest of the day was mine to do as I wished, until supper-time at 1900. Needing no further bidding, I changed into unaccustomed civvies and, for the first time in three months, left the ship. After constant motion associated with a supertanker, walking along a stationary jetty for the initial few steps seemed quite strange, but adjustment was soon made to the feel of firm ground underfoot. A short trip took me into Tenby, and with the novelty of wandering around shops I bought a few pieces of recorded classical music to enliven the next voyage. Inevitably my sojourn ended up in the main hotel, where a very leisurely slap-up lunch, preceded by a schooner of sherry and accompanied by a bottle of wine, was thoroughly enjoyed. Once the staff discovered my immediate seafaring background, they proved very obliging. They led me to their comfortable residents' lounge for coffee and left me between attempting completion (optimistically) of *The Times* crossword, snoozing, and generally relaxing. Returning to the ship via the library and seafront, a taxi ended my perfect, unexpected out-of-the-ordinary day.

After relieving Douggie at 2000 hrs, while performing the by now routine duties opening gas vents and suction valves, I was left to conclude somewhat ruefully that my holiday was well and truly over. This was not with any regrets but a certain feeling of satisfaction and near familiarity. Even though there remained much for me to learn, I started to believe that perhaps Derek might be right on yet another account: I was on the verge of developing into 'a real tanker man'. We commenced discharge conveniently at 2350 just as Paul took over the cargo watch, and two days later completed all cargo. With the ship correctly ballasted and tugs and pilot raring to go, we sailed. Captain Agnew put me in charge aft without Paul for our departure, which passed without problems.

Similar to meeting storm-force winds, fog was a common hazard encountered anywhere in the world. Frequently this was so dense it was not possible to sight visually ahead of the ship. Apart from calling the master to the bridge and putting the engines on standby, both radars were activated and an extra lookout called to see any objects that might be missed by the radars. (Ray Solly)

The log book entry declared once again: '*Rania Chandris* was bound from Angle Bay towards PGFO (Persian Gulf for Orders).' But, as we cleared the St Govan light vessel to pass off Lundy Island, the master came onto the bridge and, with his customary whimsical smile, told me to alter the ship's destination. We were to call into Brest and change both our flag and the crew! This interesting news came at an inappropriate moment as our ship was proceeding in dense fog with a build-up of shipping over a number of directions. I had already phoned him to advise the rapid decrease in visibility and ask him to pop into the wheelhouse, but had not received an answer. Instinctively, I had already been working the main radar, so I switched on the secondary, checked the position of the ship from the totally reliable Decca 1B SW Britain chain and radar, and called Geordie to take the helm, with my standby man to come to the wheelhouse for lookout duties. Luckily, as I sounded the regulation signal for vessels under way in restricted visibility, my thankful reflection was that, following their previous maintenance, our electronic gear was now working well.

CHAPTER FIVE

THE MONSTER APPEASED

As the watch continued, the fog lifted and the traffic slackened, Captain Agnew elaborated on his bombshell news. It seemed the company had experienced some sort of dispute with the British Shipping Federation and, along with various other machinations to which we were not party, had decided to re-register all its fleet of VLCCs to the Liberian flag, consistent with its other two fleets. It had also arranged for the European crew to leave the vessel, as we would subsequently sail with a deck department of Indians, with Goanese catering ratings under their Butler, and Pakistan ratings in the engine room. The Asian crew were due to arrive the next day and would be accommodated locally until our English ratings had left the vessel. Meanwhile, we would change our flag, log book, certification, and port of registration aft.

Geordie and the bosun were absolutely livid. It seemed they had decided serving aboard *Rania Chandris* was not so unpleasant after all, not that this meant much, and accordingly the next morning after breakfast they left the ship aboard a local ferry boat.

I was on anchor watch and waved them a cheery farewell from the starboard bridge wing, which was actually acknowledged seemingly devoid of rancour. Within an hour our Asian crew had arrived from the same port launch. They quickly boarded the ship, and we junior officers left it to the seniors to help them settle into the vessel. Captain Agnew had always sailed with European crews, so asked a number of questions regarding my thoughts on sailing with what would be totally new personnel. I suggested that generally they were excellent regarding ordinary duties, that I had always found them reliable, invariably very well behaved and rarely interested in alcohol, but would possibly need more numbers than a European crew for many deck duties, and they would watch closely the behaviour and actions of their officers during any emergencies.

It would be true to say that while our engines were not breaking completely down so regularly, they still emitted occasional voices of protest. The first we on bridge watch were aware of any particular problem was initiated by a phone call from the duty engineering officer advising a reduction in revolutions, followed rapidly by precisely that, which lasted for varying periods ranging from half an hour to two or three. Sometimes we were brought to a complete halt, drifting with current, for lengthy periods.

It was good to settle to regular watch-keeping routines with my customary two to three hours of deck work. Certainly, I was gaining considerable confidence in performing my 'tanker duties' but, as ever at sea, was careful not to allow these to become familiar. On this trip, the passage between Brest and Cape Town passed without incident, notwithstanding a slight personal shudder as we passed off Sierra Leone. My secunny (quartermaster) and Lascari 1 standby men were superb: typically easy to work with and completely trustworthy. Captain Agnew mentioned only casually that he found it 'rather strange for a while becoming accustomed to a different work ethic', a euphemism I regarded as delightfully dry, but let pass without comment!

During those welcome moments each day when he popped up into the wheelhouse during my evening watches for a shared cup of ship's cocoa and, increasingly frequently when he joined me in the wheelhouse for morning coffee, I became fascinated discussing with the master what developed into a series of routine chats. Many patterns concerning intimacies of my new trade were learnt that could never be gleaned so comprehensively from books or my own research.

Often, topics for these sessions began quite casually while working together on the main deck and one particular subject arose when we were releasing yet another stuck tank content measuring gauge at number three centre. It was not raining, but the morning was dull and overcast with the ship pitching and rolling heavily in a typically North Atlantic weather system. I had been instructed the previous day to adjust our course and come off track while we steamed 70 miles from Land's End to discharge 80 tons of water and waxy sediment from both slop tanks. This cargo residue had been pumped into these special tanks following discharge of crude oil a few days earlier in Europoort and Coryton.

I had felt some disquiet over this task, but being new both to trade and captain had not felt sufficiently confident then to raise what I thought might be a delicate issue. This did not stop me taking advantage of an appropriate moment to raise the question. Captain Agnew shot me a rather pensive glance, but then offered his typically comprehensive explanation.

The reasons, it seemed, were rooted in days following the Second World War. It appeared this conflict had given something more than merely a military shake-up to the world's governing authorities. For it was from 1945 that concerns became expressed regarding the damage caused to virtually all oceans, seas and rivers by numerous forms of pollution. Assorted waste of vast magnitudes was being poured into rivers, which inevitably reached the seas from industrial sites, factories and car engine oils that were poured into the world's numerous drainage systems, and of course from ships at sea. The greatest damage from the latter source was oil residue discharge from tankers.

The United States government gave a lead in 1948 with its Water Pollution Control Act designed for local agricultural and domestic use to clean up drinking water. Their motion had been adopted in 1954 by the UK government introducing its own Oil Pollution Regulations, which had (eventually) been ratified internationally by the newly instituted International Maritime Consultative Organisation (IMCO). This had been established in Geneva in 1948, but its 172 members and three associates met for the first time at their London headquarters in 1959 to discuss establishing a framework of comprehensive regulations concentrating specifically on mammoth issues of safety at sea and environmental pollution.

Repercussions from the horrific pollution caused by the *Torrey Canyon* grounding in 1967, when 120,000 tons of crude oil poured onto Cornish and French beaches, finally and irrevocably focused minds in the international maritime community. Seemingly, after lengthy and convoluted negotiations, agreement was finally reached between flag-state signatories to the setting up and accepting of Annexes One and Two of the Marine Pollution Protocols of 1973, respectively covering prevention of pollution by oil and noxious liquid substances, just one year before I joined *Rania Chandris*. These protocols were later amended in 1978 to appear notionally as MARPOL73/78.

Basically, it became approved for tankers to pump out polluted water when they were not less than 50 miles from the nearest land, as long as the discharge was limited to a maximum 100 parts of oil for each million litres. It was, of course, still not an ideal arrangement but was a perfectly accepted legal practice – even if ethical considerations strongly affected the consciences of numerous responsible mariners. But as a keen learner of my trade, it was good to be actively involved at the ground level of the procedures covering such positive practices.

It seemed that while the tasks themselves were comparatively straightforward to implement, these international wheels ground unbelievably slowly, largely due to difficulties in obtaining agreement across all member nations. This slowed the process of agreement considerably. Seemingly, it was only through the unbelievably patient persistence of the International Maritime Organisation (IMO, which was to replace the IMCO in 1982) that success was or would be achieved. Their wheels ground extremely slowly but thoroughly, but even so all protocols advocated by remaining parts of MARPOL73/78 would experience rumblings and not be fully ratified (apart from some concerning the acceptance of air pollution controls) until the early twenty-first century. Slow wheels indeed.

★ ★ ★

Social life aboard these monsters was largely home-made. True, we had films suitable for projecting on screens that were shared with the European ratings. They used their own facilities in the crew mess room. There was a wide variety of subjects, including the ever popular who-dunnits, adventures where the star managed to get himself into and remove himself and his female paramour from unbelievably impossible situations. It was interesting though, while on watch in tropical waters with a vista of stars overhead, hearing the dulcet tones of a Western hero battling with Indians and bandits in exciting situations. Frequently, the master joined us for the film and we often discussed what passed for the plot over coffee next morning. I hear still his opening gambit: 'What did you think of the *fillum* last evening, Mr Solly?' and our mutual chuckles as we dissected and offered our own equally as impossible alternatives to that dreamed up by the producer.

Games of 'snooker' (using pucks) and darts were ideal ways in which all officers joined in to relax on board. Differences of rank were frequently cast into the background as senior officers mixed with cadets and junior officers. (Both BP plc)

Invariably, time was spent in the officer's own cabin studying a diversity of subjects, or working for entries in popular Marine Society competitions, and merely reading local newspapers. But undoubtedly, the most favoured hour of the day was after coming off watch and settling to the sheer delight of a pre-sleep read. (BP plc)

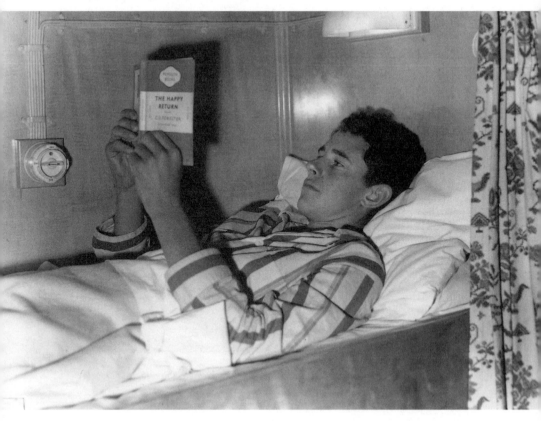

There was a lot of laughter aboard. Officers of all departments relaxed in the lounge sharing jokes and often our own versions of 'singalongs'. These were known universally in the Merchant Navy as Ships' Officers Dramatic Society events, or colloquially SODS Operas, as we sung what ashore would be called rugby songs, often with home-made tunes to which the more ingenious officer could make up verses as we passed these among us as rounds. The verses were in the form of simple limericks and one I recall for its subtlety went:

There was a young man of Bengal
Who had a mathematical ball.
The sum of its weight was pie-cubed
Over eight, plus three times
The square root of bugger all.

Chats in the duty mess were always relaxed and friendly, where officers of all departments could mix, sharing breaks at appropriate moments in between duties in the wheelhouse, engine or radio rooms. (BP plc)

For quieter moments, sharing a drink, chat about family or even occasional work matters and fighting over the chessboard in each other's cabins helped provide variety. Aboard this VLCC, my protagonist, the senior third engineer, and I enjoyed many a chess battle. We were roughly evenly matched but learnt a great deal from each other's tactics (and errors). (BP plc)

The more musically talented officers brought away guitars, which were by this time well in fashion and making significant contributions towards our enjoyment. Just chatting at the bar also passed away our social hours convivially, as well as chats in the duty mess for coffee in between duties in the engine room or on deck.

★ ★ ★

After lunch and supper, officers retired to the smoke room, where coffee was served. Those occasions after the evening meal were particularly valuable: the captain, chief and second engineers along with Derek and day work engineers mingled with off-duty watch keepers before adjourning to the bar for casual drinks or games of cards and darts, or even to someone's cabin for a modest SODS Opera. This was the time when anecdotes covering ships and seamen worldwide were exchanged that never graced books or family reunions ashore. Some of these proved very enlightening and at times vaguely disturbing, but their veracity 'stood as they stood' as it were, for most of us were sufficiently nautically *au fait* to recognise if any nautical wool was being pulled over our eyes.

One such story was related by the second engineer that occurred when he was serving with a leading dry-cargo ship company on the Far Eastern run that certainly had a ring of breathtaking truth. It seemed that this particular ship had taken on a new Chinese crew in Hong Kong during a routine crew change. What was not routine was the apparent communist agitator that had been imported from further north among the four engine room fitters. These were generally 'not only good people, but superb at their work and the equal of any junior engineering officer', according to the second.

As all Chinese crews, regardless of department, tended to keep themselves to themselves, the first officers became aware of potential problems was when the serang started passing indirect comments to the second that things were happening within his crew that were becoming far from normal. This spread when the agitator began creating difficulties with duty engineers, largely unrest that spread close to insubordination, but insufficient to justify a 'logging', the way in which the Merchant Navy deals with offences of indiscipline. The serang had done his best to pacify the situation, aided by his petty officers, but without any positive effect. It seemed that things were approaching a stage where continuous wrangling was causing unrest among the other ratings, like 'water dripping away at a stone', as the situation was described. When the chief passed on to the Old Man his fears, the latter offered to have a timely word, but the chief declined this, preferring to wait until the cleaner did something for which severe action might be justified, and then take him to the bridge. It seemed that the situation was left in limbo. The agitator continued agitating and the officers and crew, unable to see any way out, continued putting up with the situation.

The first anyone became aware of a problem was when the second officer was stood down from his watch at around 0500 hrs and relieved by the chief mate to attend a rating who had slipped down the engine room access ladder. When he arrived he found one of the fitters crumpled up and groaning. It seemed the fitter was the communist agitator. There was the possibility of a broken ankle, judging by the swollen, discoloured limb and pain, so he immediately organised his removal via the Neilson stretcher to the ship's hospital for further examination. Drills with 'Fred the dummy' on that ship seemed to have produced dividends. The Old Man came to the sickbay and between him and the second mate did all they could to make the man comfortable. After the master had left, he told Sparks to contact shore and arrange hospitalisation when the ship docked in the Australian port of Perth next day.

It was while the second officer was looking after his patient that the fitter expressed his belief that someone had oiled the handrails and steps for the middle portion of about five steps and it was this that had caused his accident. The poor old second was left to deal with a very dangerous accusation, but acted wisely by telling the man to report his suspicions to the chief, while he would inform the captain.

From there things began to hum. It was impossible to keep this news quiet, so speculation among the officers was delightfully rife. It certainly

took their minds off excessive heat on a ship in which the air conditioning had broken down. This, at least to us aboard *Rania Chandris*, gave the
story a very authentic ring. Seemingly, the consensus on board the cargo
ship was 'that a certain viscous substance was about to hit the fan with an
almighty vengeance'. Admittedly, it seemed, the junior engineers joined
the mates expressing the unspoken and secret thought that just possibly
there might have been a 'little enemy action down below'. The captain
and chief apparently went into conclave for a while, aware that the police
would have to join the ambulance crew on the jetty.

Eventually, the fitter was despatched to hospital, leaving the police to
interview all those remotely associated with the man's accusations. They
took detailed statements, which agreed with entries in the official log book,
for placing before a magistrate. It was with bated breath that this august
official's verdict was awaited. When it came it was something of an anti-
climax. This was to the effect that there was no evidence to support the
accusation made by the fitter, that rails and ladders in the engine room
accesses were bound to be oily and slippery, and that a seafarer of his experience should have exercised more care when using them. This document
was inserted along with others in the log book, subsequently to be handed
over to the appropriate authority when the ship returned to Honkers. Thus
the matter ended, but what a field day for conjecture … then and since!

*Sharing a drink in the bar and an occasional musical evening were opportunities for all officers to
meet and relax. Again, differences in rank when on duty were shelved and generally a necessary
break from work was enjoyed by all officers. (Both Athel Line)*

It is probably worth re-emphasising that relaxing in the privacy of our own cabins, when afforded a 'catching up of breath time', made these periods of solitude the more valuable for that. A strong image that still tickles my memory bank is listening to the BBC's Overseas Programme with its interruptions as the music faded and reappeared consistent with local static, and of course the staccato song of Morse as Sparks kept us in touch with the distant (in more ways than one) wider world. It would be true to say that in between ports most of us lived almost in a vacuum, aggravated (if that is the right word) by the isolationist life of tankers where most refineries were miles away from civilisation, making shore leave a virtual impossibility. But this is what living was like socially aboard these monsters in the 1970s. Without nostalgia, I still recall these moments upon swallowing the anchor and coming ashore permanently. I suppose navigation and collision avoidance were those of my duties most missed, along as a close second, the unparalleled social life and transitory friendships established and enjoyed aboard most of the ships upon which I served.

★ ★ ★

Meanwhile, more prosaically, professional life had to go on, and a totally new thing for me to learn was the extended process of tank cleaning. This commenced once we cleared Las Palmas and entered warmer waters – warm water next to the wing-tanks of our single-hulled ship made clearing the oil sludge from the tank that much easier.

Crude oil, as it settled after discharge and stripping, left sand and waxy asphalt-like substances that remained as very thick sediment on the sides and bottom of the tanks, colloquially known as 'sludge'. This had to be removed, otherwise it would eventually block pipes and valves. The extra weight also reduced payload considerably as a VLCC of our capacity could amass an undesirable 15cm, representing around 6 per cent or 2,000 tons of bill of lading cargo capacity. There was an additional problem. The tanks with their residue of oil cargo contained a mixture of different levels of hydrocarbon gases, which remained highly toxic and inflammable. As the sludge lay dormant within the tank, it generated its own gas pockets within the mass that prevented it vaporising. This meant great care had to be exercised during its removal. The gas was extremely dangerous. It possessed little smell so the first a crew member became aware that he might be subjected to its effects was a gradual feeling of tiredness. That was the time to bail out of the tank as quickly as possible.

Very powerful rotating jets of the cleaning machines were used to start the tank-cleaning operation and these directed cool or heated water around the tanks according to the descending grade of oil from heavy to lighter. Single- or double-nozzle cleaning machines were inserted through the water-tight aperture on the main deck (colloquially called Butterworth hatches after the brand name of a leading manufacturer). These were lowered through a series of about five drops, for between thirty to forty-five minutes duration per drop, each emitting jets of water under very high pressure that impinged over virtually all of each tank. Initially aboard *Rania Chandris*, we cleaned sufficient tanks into which the dirty waste could be pumped until there was enough to pass into the slop tanks port and starboard at the after end of number five wings. It was, alas, this residue that was initially pumped into the seas.

It was then time for the interesting operation commonly known as 'tank diving'. But first, the chief or duty officer would descend into the tank, monitoring as far as a possible gas safety levels. Once these had been deemed safe, the crew, armed with mucking winches, portable gantries, rubber buckets and shovels to prevent sparking, descended to the tank bottom and commenced the filthy job of clearing away the sludge. The resulting scale had then to be winched by hand 94.2ft (28.7m) to the main deck. It was then also dumped into the ocean, so adding its own unwelcome contribution towards world sea pollution. Once the tanks had been cleaned, powerful fans were introduced to dry them, after which Derek, accompanied by one of the other mates, inspected the results of their labours while preparing to do the same operation with port authorities prior to loading the next cargo.

Above left: Sludge was the residue of the crude oil cargo left following discharge. This was often as much as 6–8in in depth and had to be removed to prevent the clogging of pipes and valves, and also to reduce weight that would otherwise be lost to cargo. (Victor Pyrate)

Above right: Inserting a manual tank cleaning machine into a cargo tank was very much an essential prelude to removal of sludge in pre-MARPOL crude oil tankers of all sizes. These emitted a high-pressure rotating jet of water at varying temperature dependent upon the temperature of the cargo. (BP plc)

Left: The deck controls for a fixed tank-cleaning machine that could be regulated to the required temperature and jet force. (Ray Solly)

Once the tank had been washed, the chief officer would check for the presence of toxic and explosive gas remaining following discharge and washing, before the crew could descend to complete cleaning the tank. Here, the chief officer is making a routine check for gas presence in the pump room using a similar type of explosimeter. A typical cargo pump is shown in the foreground. (BP plc)

Once the tanks had been washed, crew and cadets under the supervision of the duty mates would descend to the bottom and commence the potentially dangerous and definitely filthy task of removing the sludge. This job was known with typical marine humour as 'tank diving'. (BP plc)

The final act of deck officers once the tanks had been cleaned and aired was to make an inspection ascertaining that they were ready in all respects for the shore surveyor to check that the ship was ready to load her next crude cargo. (Victor Pyrate)

★ ★ ★

Working on deck, enjoying the heat of a tropical sun with the smooth calm seas drifting idly past the vessel, was an image that remains engraved onto my mind. It seemed to epitomise the relaxed manner in which my duties now seemed to be undertaken. I was still overwhelmed by the size of this monster ship, but no longer intimidated by her. I felt at one with all aspects of my job, my colleagues, and myself. It was with eager anticipation that I subjected myself to the fully professional training patiently offered by my seniors in the numerous roles associated with my new calling.

I was on the bridge for arrival at Ras Tanura and immediately afterwards onto the cargo deck watch. Once I had the gangway fixed and arranged for my quartermaster, or secunny, to be in attendance, my next job was the important task of supervising the discharge of dirty ballast water. This had been taken in designated cargo tanks outward bound to increase the stability of the vessel during a severe storm experienced up coast off Beira. I was able to exercise some control over the task by simply watching carefully until the merest trace of oil appeared, and then quickly informing the duty engineer officer, who immediately ceased discharge. Another lesson automatically imbibed was the extent of co-operation between deck and engineering officers aboard tankers of this class. There was no longer any of the often far from subtle departmental warfare that had been found to be an encroachment to harmonious relationships as some voyages aboard dry-cargo ships developed.

A scene forever associated in my mind with VLCCs and reminiscent of the peace and tranquillity associated with these ships was drifting serenely through cloudless, calm tropical seas while engaged on some form of gentle deck work. (Ray Solly)

I was aware that loading and discharging cargoes entailed considerably more technical expertise than that to which I was a party. For example, even I was learning from the sidelines, as it were, the vital need for accurate assessments to be made monitoring stresses and strains on a ship's hull. I had discussed with Derek the loading computer that he used diligently, but was well aware that for the time being I was not to be made a party to such deeper information until I had further experience under my belt and could appreciate better the physical and chemical properties of the cargo and effects of these on the ship. So, quite happy in this knowledge, I took my own third officer's role in all duties at Ras Tanura.

On this voyage, we went to anchorage for two days, during which we deck officers kept the usual anchor watch. This entailed retaining a close eye on our position but, as we were on one hour's notice of readiness, making sure that we did not miss any radio calls from the shore advising the onset of pilot and tugs. The engines were kept on standby, which meant that those below also kept routine sea watches.

It had to be at 0200 that we received the summons for berthing and in a flurry of movement, pilot and tugs arrived to bring us alongside. I was again with Paul down aft to bring the vessel alongside, while Douggie was sent forward to gain experience of the first officer's role, leaving Derek to observe him from the wheelhouse and do the third mate's job. I appreciated Captain Agnew's enthusiastic approach to training his officers for their next step upwards on the promotion ladder. While observing events taking place as third officer on this particular occasion, Derek – to his delight – was often called to the bridge in addition to the duty mate to observe and discuss with the pilot and master bringing the VLCC alongside jetties and to anchorage. On this occasion, I supervised the operation while Paul stood apart and supervised me: we managed between us to bring the vessel alongside without any disasters.

We had an abrupt halt to proceedings for an hour while the engines misbehaved and had to be given extra tender loving care to coax sufficient life from them so they could continue the operation of bringing us into position off the berth. Once the ship was lined up correctly, and Paul and I had just put the first line ashore, there was an abrupt halt to proceedings. Over the VHF, with a slight trace of humour in his voice, Derek advised there was a power failure ashore. With seven tugs straining to hold us in position alongside against a fairly fast current, there was little we could do but wait. The delay lasted just under forty minutes when, to the relief of us all, we were given permission to proceed.

Working aft amidst such an expansive space was a strange sensation as I supervised my crew putting ashore a breast rope, while Paul put out a second back spring. These warps kept the vessel fast alongside and released the tugs while we put out the remaining stern lines. When we were finally made fast, I was stood down to appear on deck after breakfast at 0800 hrs, taking over from Douggie in continuing the six-hour task of discharging ballast, between taking draft and ullages. At 2000 I returned on deck and was left alone to get on with loading the vessel. We were taking cargo at 20,000 tons per hour using all four cargo pumps. This proved quite a steady watch manipulating valves according to Derek's loading plan and the ubiquitous task of taking ullages. I was also aware of adhering to port safety instructions and keeping an eye on my quartermaster and a Lascari 2 (or second-class sailor) as his assistant as they attended our moorings.

A slight list to port was noticed after an hour into my watch and this increased before my eyes from 2½ degrees to 3 in ten minutes. Well aware that this was a moment for sole decision, I closed port wing tanks one, two and three to see how this affected the trim. It did not seem to make much difference, so thirty minutes later I closed the remaining wing tanks port and starboard, leaving only the slops open. As the list decreased, I half-opened port wings one, two and three, which reduced the list to 1 degree, and then opened fully the remaining wing tanks. The entire task was a largely a case of thinking on my feet and observing closely the effects my actions were making. It paid off for, by the end of the watch as I handed over to my relief, the vessel was on an even keel. Apart from the diligent duty engineering officer, who made no comment, only I was aware of the situation and how this had been handled. I offer the example as a typical incident that, significantly, had been handled correctly, giving a much-needed monumental boost to my confidence.

In the latter part of my morning watch next day I worked with Derek on deck topping off all wing tanks and taking ullages and draft in preparation for our departure. At 1630 my traditional third officer duties in the wheelhouse for our departure from Ras Tanura were taken up. My final task was to take a draft all round and we left port with a mean of 46ft 4in.

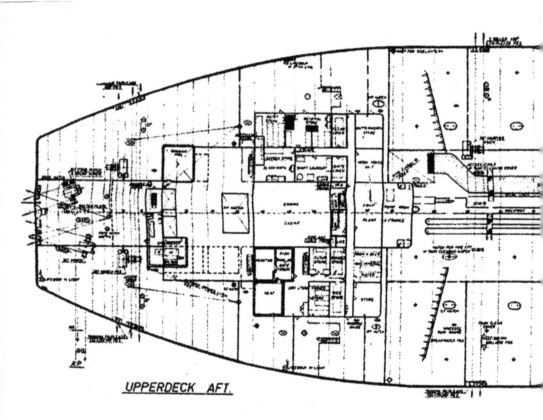

UPPERDECK AFT.

The after deck of Rania Chandris *offered a far greater space for observation and crew control during mooring operations than that found on the conventional dry-cargo ship. The positions of winches and bollards for taking tugs are clearly visible.*

Cadets flaking out an 8in mooring rope forward in preparation for this to be run out over a winch drum. (BP plc)

Above left: *Usually three turns of a mooring rope were run over the winch drum, conventional to all ships regardless of capacity or cargo. (BP plc)*

Above right: *The* British Respect *is in her final stages of being brought alongside her berth at the port of Lavéra in France. (BP plc)*

Taking the ropes ashore. These were usually run out onto the deck of a mooring boat and brought alongside the jetty. The head of a boatman is just visible in the LLHS. (BP plc)

Mooring winch with wire crossing the main deck to the starboard side aft of the midships jetty. A polypropylene mooring rope has been singled up for departure awaiting later stowing in the locker. These were a vast improvement over the previously used sisals, but when wet were extremely heavy to handle. (Ray Solly)

A typical view taken during a mooring operation aft aboard Rania Chandris. *A wire is seen run out across the main deck to the starboard side jetty with a rope made fast to bollards. Berthing operations aboard these large VLCCs are invariably taken at a leisurely pace compared to dry-cargo vessels and coasters. (Ray Solly)*

A page taken from a deck working book during a typical cargo loading operation. Ullages are taken hourly, and as both wing tanks are loaded the decrease in tank space is clearly seen. The 2305 hrs entry relates to the final stages of an adjustment to the vessel's trim following correction of an earlier list.

It took just a few hours for us make the run to, and bring the vessel up to, anchorage at Mina al Ahmadi. Here we were scheduled to complete loading all centre tanks with a heavier grade of crude oil. This was a straightforward loading of 110,000 tons crude that took until 0700, when hoses were disconnected. No time was wasted on this trip for by 0800 pilot and tugs were in position and, once clear of the berth with pilot and all but one tug away, under the master's orders we entered the 35-mile-long approach channel. Again, I was on the bridge for this departure.

CHAPTER SIX

AN INDULGENCE OF INCIDENTS

As we were approaching the African coast chugging along quite happily enjoying an uneventful voyage, our equanimity was shaken slightly. I had handed over the watch to Paul and had been turned in for about an hour, so was in that initially deep state of sleep when, ordinarily, it would have taken a stick of dynamite to awaken me. And indeed the shudder that made the ship stumble in her track could indeed well have been explosive. Befogged with sleep for a few seconds, my mind went into overdrive and for a split second I wondered if we had been involved in a collision, but with mind awakening rapidly, I realised that was not possible. Glancing at the clock and seeing the time was shortly after 0500 hrs, I realised there had been no other ships anywhere in the vicinity when leaving the bridge. In the early (even optimistic) hope of a navigational early landfall, I had switched on the main radar, noticing instinctively the nearest ship to our own was 50 miles away beyond the extreme 48-mile edge of the screen: she was well astern and going on an opposite course! Meanwhile, our ship had picked herself up. Her engines and motion through the water seemed normal, so whatever had called me from my bunk had not proved fatal to the vessel.

In the few seconds it had taken my mind to work through those natty pieces of logic, I was wide awake, fully dressed in working uniform and on my way to the wheelhouse.

Captain Agnew was already there in animated discussion with the chief officer. They glanced up as I rounded the chart area and asked them if there was anything I could do. Derek responded with his usual whimsical smile, but the master told me that they had no idea what had happened, but were discussing possibilities. I could take a torch and the VHF set and set out along the port side of the main deck checking everything topside on route, while the second officer would take the starboard side and do likewise. By this time, bleary eyed and still slightly befuddled with sleep, Douggie had joined us.

My search revealed that everything was apparently in order with no visible signs of damage. Meeting with Paul in the eyes of the ship, we notified the bridge and compared notes, not that the latter took very long! After meandering down the near quarter-of-a-mile-long catwalk, checking manifolds and cross-over pipes en route, we returned our gear to the bridge and were stood down by the master. The chief engineer meanwhile had checked everything in his various domains with the same results as ourselves. There was no mistaking the fact that the ship had experienced a massive explosion somewhere, but we were all totally mystified concerning what might have happened, and where. On that rather downcast note, we were both stood down to continue what remained of our broken slumbers.

With my seniority as third officer confirmed recently in a very belated message from Captain Branch, the master agreed I could be relied on to take accurate morning sights and to check and wind the chronometers. This meant Paul was relieved of these essential tasks so he could work with Derek and come later onto the bridge for noon sights. Assuming he passed the exams, it was good training for his promotion to another VLCC in the fleet as chief officer. On this occasion when I popped up to share a tray of afternoon tea and biscuits and have a social chat, he was all agog with the importance of acquired knowledge and clearly eager to impart this to an ignorant acolyte, so enthusiastically he solved the mystery of our 'bang in the night', as I had ruefully termed the incident. After I had relieved him of his watch at 0800 hrs, Derek followed a hunch that had come to him while taking an amplitude of the sun to check for possible errors in the magnetic compass. Before shooting off to breakfast, he had popped into the pump room entrance immediately below the accommodation block 'just to check'. Faced with nearly 100ft of dirty water swirling around the ladder top leading to the pumps, he had solved the mystery. It seemed one of our main ballast pumps had exploded with such force that it had flooded the compartment. For the next few days, our task when on deck work was to assist Derek supervising the crew cleaning the entire area – once of course the engineers had pumped the room dry. Between us, we used our entire stock of Permoglaze cleaning fluid and cloths. The reason why it had exploded with such violence was never answered but this did not stop us bandying around numerous possible theories, along with even more impossible ones – some admittedly bordering on the bizarre!

★ ★ ★

I relieved Douggie as we passed off East London and as a reflex action checked the ship's position. This was not done to check up in any way on the officer I had relieved but, for the prudent navigator aboard any vessel, was fulfilment of the fact that I was now responsible to the master for the safety of the ship over the next four hours. I took bearings and checked the radar and Decca Navigator, the latter of which was pretty reliable on this part of the east African coast. I plotted my position and found it put the vessel just under 10 miles off the coast. Rechecking the set and drift of the Agulhas current, it appeared that Douggie, in his infinite wisdom and professional experience, had failed to take its effect into consideration. This was technically quite serious as the South African government had decreed all tankers should keep a minimum of 12 miles off its coastline, so we were 2 miles inside our course line. The only option open was to lay off a new course line that would bring us back gradually onto that laid off on our chart. This was not a simple matter of just putting the helm hard a starboard and bringing us back that way. After all, we were not a Mini Minor but a

300,000-ton fully laden VLCC. As it happened, it took two hours before we were lined up correctly and I could readjust our course.

About thirty minutes later, I heard the Old Man pop into the wheelhouse for his usual cup of ship's cocoa that, in the custom of the service, was so thick that it almost needed a knife and fork to drink! I heard his sharp intake of breath as he looked at the chart, and braced myself for the explosion as he came around to the wheelhouse front. Inevitably, with this man, his response was expressed quietly and in measured tones. 'Oh my goodness, Mr Solly. What happened when you took over the watch this evening?'

'Well, it was quite simple really, sir. I found the ship out of position so had to rework the course line.'

'Hmm. You had best leave this one with me.' End of saga, but I heard later from Paul (that perpetual source of all information) that poor old Douggie received something of a blistering!

Just as the vessel entered the Bay of Biscay, we received our berthing orders. On this occasion we were to call into Lyme Bay on the south coast of England and engage in a ship-to-ship transfer operation of sufficient cargo to enable us to enter the Dover Strait and proceed hence to Europoort for partial discharge before popping across to Coryton on the River Thames for completion. Following Chandris's normal practices, our 'team' would then be signed off the ship and proceed on leave for the duration of one voyage, around two months, before re-joining the tanker before she sailed for her next voyage. Inevitably, this meant changes in the 'team' as those up for further certificates would remain ashore on study leave to be replaced by new officers.

Lightening into a smaller tanker to reduce draught, enabling the larger ship to make a transit of otherwise restricted waters, is a normal VLCC operation. It usually occurs in a sheltered bay such as Lyme Bay off the south Devon coast with both ships initially under way. Were this to be attempted while one was anchored then the momentum of the approaching vessel would cause both ships to swing around the anchor.

We had rung end of passage at 0700 hrs, so that when I came on watch next day at 0800 we were steering 022 degrees (T) 10 miles East of Berry

Head. Following the master's instructions, I made first VHF contact with our lightening tanker, *Esso Cardiff*, ten minutes afterwards. By agreement, I commenced a gradual alteration to our course, bringing the VLCC to 270 degrees (T) and reducing speed to 4 knots, allowing the lightening vessel to come alongside. These specialist tankers are very distinctive for they have along the length of the main deck four large 'Swettenham' fenders set in special derricks. We took the first lines from *Esso Cardiff* at 0922 hrs and one hour later both ships were made fast alongside. A few minutes later we let go and were brought up to our port anchor with six shackles in the water. I took anchor bearings visually and confirmed these by radar fixes and Decca Navigator, leaving both tankers lying quietly to anchor, but in a gale force 8 westerly wind. Until I was stood down to have lunch at 1200 hrs, these bearings were checked frequently.

A Swettenham fender was the distinctive mark of a tanker of around 60,000sdwt used to lighten a larger VLCC. Four of these were placed along the main deck housed in specially constructed derricks. (BP plc)

Left: *The smaller tanker came alongside the laden VLCC at a speed around 4kn with the Swettenham fenders lowered into position. (BP plc)*

Below: *Here the* British Dragoon *lies alongside a fellow BP VLCC with fenders lowered, derricks raised and gangway in position. The manifold connections have been made and the cargo is ready to be pumped. (BP plc)*

Both ships are equal in height as the cargo is pumped from the VLCC into the lightening tanker, showing the transfer operation nearing completion. (BP plc)

Stepping out on deck afterwards, I attended and opened number three manifolds and then Derek asked me to take over in the cargo control room for and during the early part of the transfer. The plan was for us to discharge 42,000 tons at a rate of 5,000 tons per hour taken from both sets of wing tanks at numbers one, three and five using cargo pumps two and three. Things went off quite smoothly and we completed the ship-to-ship transfer by 2130 hrs, so both ships were away on their respective courses within fifteen minutes. Before going on watch, I worked the crew shipping our starboard derrick and generally squaring off on deck as necessary. I finally returned to the bridge at 2300 hrs for the final hour of my watch.

Our reduced mean draught of 63ft 6in proved adequate for our arrival off Le Havre light vessel at 0930 hrs next day. This was an unexpected port of call, but consistent with the unpredictable nature of VLCC trading. We then spent two hours cruising between the light vessel and

Seine Banks awaiting a pilot. It took the usual seven tugs and a further four hours to turn us around in the New Basin and bring us alongside Number 10 berth in the New Sea Basin.

I was back in the wheelhouse for this standby while Paul went forward with Derek, leaving Douggie to go aft. In an unguarded moment over coffee in the lounge afterwards, he admitted to me that he found working aft in these vast spaces was disquieting as he felt 'too old a dog to learn new tricks'. I could only help by reassuring him of my own awareness of the same problem, but I was left feeling as we left the lounge that neither of us was really convinced!

★ ★ ★

An understandingly benevolent fate allowed the challenges of transiting the Dover Strait to fall firmly within my watch. Immediately after I relieved Douggie and before he had closed the wheelhouse door, it was time for me to alter course and take Le Basurelle light vessel off the port beam at a distance of 3.2nm. This significant waypoint indicated the northwards turn out of the English Channel into the Dover Strait, geographically roughly off the port of Le Tréport.

An hour later we passed the light off the Cape of Alprech at 7.8nm, when I gave Captain Agnew a phone call: 'We have just passed Alprech, sir, and are on course for Cap Gris-Nez. The traffic situation in the separation zones ahead is quite heavy with the usual run of cross-Channel ferries, a few fishing boats and pleasure craft, but no potential problems at the moment. I am just going to contact VHF CROSSMA (the French traffic control authority) and have notified Dover Coastguard Channel Navigation Service of our restricted draught, cargo, destination and intentions. They have already added us to their navigation safety broadcasts.' As courteous as ever, he acknowledged my call and advised 'he was on his way'.

Our intention was to navigate the VLCC within the deepest water available consistent with, on this occasion, our 60ft (18m) draught, but in subsequent trips we made the same passage drawing the maximum of 72ft (22m). While obviously mindful of our obligations under the International Collision Regulations, we were unable to manoeuvre outside the deep-water channel – something unthinkable with between 50 and 80 million gallons of crude oil on board! Even a lateral displacement to our course of half-a-mile was difficult to contemplate, so we could not give way to crossing ferries, yachts or cabin cruisers, or determine those unfathomably erratic courses steered frequently by trawlers as they chased shoals of fish around the oceans. We had to stand on and rely on other craft to give way to our international deep-draught signal.

I had already given the master's steward a bell advising him to take a tray of tea and toast to the captain's cabin. The Decca was its usual totally reliable self, and came in well with visual and radar checks on the ship's position. Even before he arrived as we passed off Boulogne, a rogue trawler of indeterminate nationality ran across our bows, giving me what is known in the trade as 'a slight palpitation'. It caused me to knock the steering off automatic and place my secunny on the helm, and I then phoned for my standby man to come to the bridge for lookout duties.

Upon his arrival, Captain Agnew surveyed the situation and took the secondary radar on the 6- to 3-mile range, monitoring targets I fed to him from my overall view on the main radar set, which I kept operational on the 12- or 6-mile range. He would then order any course alterations necessary. Meanwhile, I continued monitoring the secunny and following Paul's suggested voyage plan. As we were so close to land, I would also 'pop a position dot' on the chart every twenty or thirty minutes depending on the demands of lookout duties both on the radar and visually. I also looked after telephones and telegraph and kept up-to-date records of our passage, while keeping one ear open for any relevant VHF messages.

Passing through the Dover Strait always proved an interesting but thoroughly enjoyable passage, for these waters were well known to me not only from pre-sea training ship days, but more significantly taking the coaster on my own through these waters in weather conditions ranging from dense fog to force 10 gusting 11 or 12 storms when the gyrocompass was thrown and my AB was placed onto the helm. Seeing these exceptionally rough seas from such a low angle, aggravated as they were by the close proximity of coastlines, was undoubtedly challenging, but the very ethos of the job proved inherently satisfying, and of course excitingly interesting. Strangely enough, there was too much upon which to concentrate for any fear to be felt, mainly because I had every confidence in both ship and able seaman. The sense of achievement allowed a host of contrasting experiences to become established deeply within my memory banks and I admitted (even then) allowing myself a perfectly happy acceptance of undoubted romanticism, combined with professionalism, blending itself within this process.

★ ★ ★

We arrived off Europoort sixteen hours later following departure from Le Havre. As forecast by radio, we anchored in 17 fathoms of water in the deep-water designated area immediately upon arrival, which was situated about 40 miles off the Hook of Holland. Although the wind was gusting westerly force 9 to 10, we lay quietly enough and were able to keep an eye on the ship's position from Decca Navigator, the position of the RY buoy 3.5nm off, and by varying the radar range.

It was 1430 hrs next day when standby was called and in a flurry of movement two pilots arrived by helicopter. Three hours later we entered Maasmond at the Hook of Holland New Waterway. Within a further three hours we were made fast starboard side alongside the VLCC jetty at No. 7 Petrolhaven and commenced cargo immediately. Instead of going on cargo watch I was stood to by the master to complete a survey form with a Lloyd's Register surveyor. This was a very thorough tally of all lifesaving equipment on board the ship and took the two of us around four hours to complete.

Our partial discharge of 83,704 tons of crude lightened the VLCC sufficiently to see us across the various Thames Estuary deep-water

Above: *Two pilots are seen safely on board a VLCC by the chief officer after having landed from a helicopter along with their own quartermaster. The 40-mile distance from the VLCC berths at Europoort more than justified this method of arrival. (BP plc)*

Left: *A VLCC lies quietly alongside her berth in Europoort. Cargo is well advanced and the connections between the ship and Chiksans on the jetty can be seen clearly. Invariably, there was always a deck man of at least AB rating on duty there to meet visitors and keep a general eye open on moorings, etc. (BP plc)*

channels lying between the Black Deep and Knock John sandbanks. I was on the bridge for much of this passage and, as our transit was made on the lowest tidal ebb, my mood ranged between interest and speculation on seeing uncovered sandbanks on both sides of the ship. Still, as the master and Thames pilot, whom we had taken on board in Europoort, seemed little perturbed, neither was I, even when our progress was hindered by a number of engine breakdowns and mishaps. As the tide caught us while ranging out of control and closing The Warp (at the lower end of our passage), even their equanimity was challenged and I heard them discussing the possibility of calling out a posse of tugs. Fortunately, the engines recovered quickly and were soon running as they should do. A few minutes later, we were called on the VHF by Thames Navigation Service at Gravesend, the port control authority advising that they had tracked our passage, noticed our gentle meandering from the course line, and enquired if all was well. Our pilot soon reassured them by VHF, and received in return a signal that because another VLCC was leaving the berth later than planned, our ship could not be taken until second high water the next day. Accordingly, we were directed to the W2 deep-water anchorage off Southend-on-Sea.

Lying quietly at anchor proved a strange experience for I had frequently passed this anchorage while going out unofficially with the Harbour Service launches *Rosherville*, *Roehampton* and the survey cutter *Havengore*, prior to becoming and as a pre-sea training deck cadet. My numerous voyages aboard dry-cargo vessels and coasters had been centred mainly on the ports of London and Medway, so this place had been passed more times than I cared to remember.

It was 0445 hrs the next morning when pilot and tugs arrived alongside to take us to the deep-water jetty at Number 4 Coryton, where a further three tugs were taken in attendance but not made fast, to keep us in position alongside the jetty. I had just twenty minutes to take a quick breakfast before going on cargo watch at 0800 and commencing discharge of all centre tanks with approximately 122,000 tons of cargo.

It was on completion of my second cargo watch that day that I was called into his cabin by Captain Agnew and issued with my second watch-keeping certificate covering both voyages with him. He announced himself pleased with my performance and the manner in which I had taken to completely new patterns of trading, and stated were I to consider doing so then at the end of my two months' leave he would be pleased to sign me on as his second officer. He was also packing in preparation to go on leave as soon as he had handed over to his relief master and advised that, owing to the unpredictable nature of VLCC trading, on returning to the ship the company booked rooms for all officers in the Hotel George in London, where they stayed until we were certain *Rania Chandris* had arrived alongside Number 4 Jetty, Coryton. By planning this advance move they made sure the ship had a full complement of navigators and engineers before minibusing them to the vessel the morning after they were sure she had made fast. My relief was on time and although new to VLCCs had recent crude and product tanker experience, having served his cadetship with London and Overseas Tanker Company. The collective move to the ship gave every-one time to readjust from a lengthy leave, meet any new officers to our teams, and prepare for the next trip. It also offered a good chance to see any London shows or theatre performances.

With two secunnies pushing the trolley with my gear aboard, we made the long walk along the causeway to meet a refinery minibus that would take me to my taxi at the gates. It was with mixed feelings that I left the vessel. Of course, I was glad to go on leave and looked forward, very much so, to meeting again with family and local areas, but I had come to feel so much part of the ship that I knew this was my way of future life. Yes, I admitted a sense of achievement. All the initial fears about taking away such a large vessel to sea and being responsible for her navigation, and brand new cargo watches, had not proved groundless but had been met head on. I knew there remained much for me to learn concerning the cargo and its associated problems of ship stability, but I looked for-ward to meeting these fresh challenges.

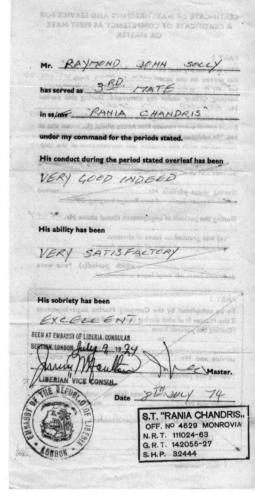

**CERTIFICATE OF WATCHKEEPING AND SERVICE FOR
A CERTIFICATE OF COMPETENCY AS FIRST MATE
OR MASTER**

PART I

This is to certify that Mr. *R. J. SOLLY* has served on the ss/mv *RANIA CHANDRIS* from *20th APR. 74* to *2st July 74* in the capacity of * (1st) (2nd) (3rd) (4th) Watch-keeping Officer under my command. During this period Mr. *RAYMOND JOHN SOLLY* was an officer in full charge of a watch for not less than *EIGHT* hours out of every twenty four hours whilst the vessel was at sea. †In addition he has regularly carried out other duties in connection with the routine and maintenance of the ship.

~~†Bridge watches were doubled during the following periods and at no other times~~

During ~~these periods Mr.~~ served ~~as the *Senior/Junior of two Bridge-keeping Officers.~~

During the periods of engagement stated above Mr. *SOLLY*

*(a) was granted no leave of absence.
~~*(b) was granted leave of absence from~~
~~to~~
~~which period(s) *was/were deducted from his total leave entitlement.~~

PART 2

To be completed by the Company Marine Superintendent if the Master is absent during the period stated.
†During the periods from ___ to ___ the vessel was on operational service and Mr. ___ was off articles.

†During the periods from ___ to ___ the vessel was laid up undergoing engine repairs and Mr. ___ was *off/on articles.

Signature of *Master/Superintendent ___

Date ___

† Delete if not applicable
* Delete as appropriate

Mr. *RAYMOND JOHN SOLLY*

has served as *3RD MATE*

in ss/mv *"RANIA CHANDRIS"*

under my command for the periods stated.

His conduct during the period stated overleaf has been

VERY GOOD INDEED

His ability has been

VERY SATISFACTORY

His sobriety has been

EXCELLENT

SEEN AT EMBASSY OF LIBERIA, CONSULAR
SECTION, LONDON *July 9* 19 *74*

LIBERIAN VICE CONSUL

___ Master.

Date *2nd JULY 74*

S.T. "RANIA CHANDRIS"
OFF. No 4629 MONROVIA
N.R.T. 111024-63
G.R.T. 142055-27
S.H.P. 32444

Above: The second certificate of watch-keeping and service (which has survived) of my first tour of duty aboard Rania Chandris *issued by the master of the vessel, confirming my role on board his VLCC as third officer.*

Below: Mobil Shipping (UK)'s VLCC Saudi Glory *was the same tonnage as* Rania Chandris *and is seen at the end of the causeway serving Number 4 Jetty Coryton on the River Thames. This was a berth often visited by both vessels as they served out a BP charter. (Ray Solly)*

Listening to my quartermasters chatting and laughing and, abstractedly, being invited to join their humour, my mood during that walk along this lengthy causeway was one of fulfilment and contentment. I knew also that Derek, who would also be re-joining us in two months' time, was correct: I did have the makings of a tanker man!

The main deck of World Unicorn. *Walking around this vast expanse of deck of this 345m, 255,600sdwt VLCC being constructed, cluttered by incomplete pipework, brought home a number of realities previously taken for granted. The houses, mostly built for shipyard workers, who doubtless enjoyed having a VLCC situated at the bottom of their garden, were equally as relieved once the vessel was launched. I found the sheer height of the deck from the accommodation block fascinating, and I tried to work out the function of a bewildering array of pipes and equipment awaiting fitting. (Swan Hunter and Wigham Richardson)*

Having walked inside the bulbous bow of Rania Chandris *during an inspection with Captain Agnew, it was interesting to see the external side of this construction being built. The figures at the bottom of the yard and on board the ship show appropriate proportions. (Swan Hunter)*

★ ★ ★

Two weeks into my leave, I received a surprise telephone call from Captain Agnew. He had arranged to visit Swan Hunter and Wigham Richardson's, the Newcastle-based ship builders, and, were I available to join him, would welcome me to gain the experience of seeing a large VLCC in its later stages of construction. I could stay with him and his wife for the couple of nights necessary to cover the trip. He had stood by as master on a number of tankers, including the VLCC *Esso Northumbria*, when these had been built by this yard and established sufficiently close links with the management for him to make this unofficial visit. With characteristic thoughtfulness, he 'thought I might be interested'.

I jumped at the chance, so two days later I was on a train heading north, where he met me at the railway station and whisked me off home. Inevitably, my welcome was most cordial and the next day we entered Swan Hunter's. Having been equipped with hard hats and appropriate gear, we were taken on board World-Wide Shipping Company's VLCC *World Unicorn*. Although not permitted to take my own photographs, the yard later kindly sent me a number of their shots as souvenirs of my trip.

The completed World Unicorn *at her launching, showing clearly the V-shaped forepart and tracing wires assisting her launching as she is held in position by an army of tugs. The ship would go from here to her fitting out berth within the yard for completion before sea trials and handing over to her owners. (Turner's Photography, Newcastle-upon-Tyne)*

CHAPTER SEVEN

CHALLENGING PROMOTION

Having been home on leave for eight weeks, I was expecting any day to receive a phone call from Captain Branch inviting my recall to the ship. After ten weeks, just as I had resolved that day to phone the good captain enquiring what was happening, he telephoned me. The reasons for the delay turned out to be quite profound. Apparently, after she had discharged her previous cargo more than two months earlier, instead of sailing for voyage number three, the relief officers received instructions to take the VLCC off charter and proceed to Rotterdam dry dock in the Botlek area. Here, to the delight of our engineering officers, she was to undergo repairs across a number of major areas including a new generator, and for the main engine to receive a 'liberal dose of good old TLC', as Paul later related he overheard the second telling the junior third engineer.

While they had the ship safely ensconced she would also have a host of areas updated that would benefit everyone, but mainly us deck officers. Paul had been phoned at home two days into his leave and offered the chance to return on board 'if he wished' prior to going on study leave, and sail with the vessel, again performing the additional second officer's duty of supervising the dry-docking. He told me when we met that he regarded this as an excellent opportunity to gain considerable experience, so he was only too glad to accept. He did not say what his wife thought about the change in plans ...

His acceptance also helped the company (and as it turned out myself) for they had been unable to find a replacement relief second officer. The guy appointed to the vessel failed to turn up at the hotel without any explanation and they had been unable to contact him before the ship sailed, so had a further reason for asking Paul to re-join. Had he refused, Captain Branch was on the verge of asking me if I would forgo my leave and re-join for one voyage in that capacity.

So instead, I joined the other officers in 'our' London hotel prior to travelling by minibus, but this time to Heathrow airport instead of the vessel so we could fly to Holland. The other good news was confirmation that I would re-join as second officer and relieve Paul before he finally went on leave just before the vessel left Rotterdam dry dock.

It was good to see Captain Agnew's smiling face as I entered the lounge of the George. Even before I was at the bar, Derek met me with a full pint of lager, welcomed me as second officer, and assured me of his wholehearted support for the forthcoming trip. I sensed Captain Agnew, as ever, just sitting back a little and watching all about him. I was pleased to see the senior third engineer and my chess protagonist had re-joined and welcomed the cheerfully stern faces of our chief and the second, although (as perhaps expected) my comment to them that they would now have some new rubber bands to play with was met with a more than blank look!

Douggie had finally 'swallowed the anchor', or retired, with his place as first officer being taken by Tim Greenway. Following his cadetship with BP and the passing of second mates, he had served subsequently with a number of American oil majors for his entire sea-going officer career. He had recently sailed as chief officer with Chevron Oil, a large United States company. I took to him immediately and eagerly accepted his offer of 'any help that you might find useful'.

In my place, we shipped a new third officer. Charles Causton had completed his cadetship with Royal Mail Lines, a dry-cargo company and, with echoes of a similar conversation ringing in my ears, had been recruited by Captain Branch 'to gain experience'. He had just failed part of his second mate examination so was brand new, carrying with him an unassuming air of charming naivety, leaving me to wonder if I also had appeared quite so when I arrived on board. I suspected the answer would prove an unequivocal yes! Studying madly, he hoped to resit the offending two papers when next he went on leave.

* * *

Once aboard, we were all amazed at the new equipment and devices that had been fitted to the vessel in such a short time of our absence. On deck, we were now proud possessors of the most recent portable gas detection monitors, and a state-of-the-art loading computer for Derek to play with, to which he promised to introduce me, once he had familiarised himself with its workings! The hydraulic pilot hoist was replaced by a ladder extension. This had arisen from a series of accidents on board other VLCCs when pilots had been injured while using the device to board and leave ships. Some men had been injured, but the final straw for IMO was when a pilot was killed. The ladder was greeted with mixed feelings. Obviously, it resulted in a safer passage but now represented an extremely long haul up the thing when these monsters were in ballast.

As by now international agreement had decreed refineries would accept the oil-water slops ashore for treatment, siphoning the final stages of sea water and recirculating the oil, we discovered an oily water separator adorning our main deck near the accommodation. We also introduced the comparatively novel 'load-on-top' system of dealing with our slops that had been originally brought to the industry by Shell International, or Shell Tankers as they were known more colloquially. This paved the way for the introduction of another delight for all officers aboard, which was the introduction of crude oil washing (COW). These innovations meant that residues of the existing cargo, after the water content had been pumped ashore, were used to wash all cargo tanks instead of water. The residue of tank washing was typically stored in the slop tanks, with the new cargo literally 'loaded on top' and merged with the new. Such small proportions, comparatively speaking, were easily assimilated without fears of contamination between grades. We deck officers breathed more than a sigh of relief, for no more would we have to supervise the crew lugging around tank-cleaning gear and follow the old time-consuming and filthy processes. It also meant a further striving towards cleaner oceans as there was now no longer any sludge to be dumped over the side.

A deck cadet opening the drain valve of an oily water separator fitted aboard a VLCC. (BP plc)

But by far the most impressive cargo improvements were the fitting of an inert gas system (IGS), which today is universally acknowledged as the greatest contribution to safety of the twentieth century aboard all tankers, irrespective of tonnage.

Before 1973, with the most basic of tank-cleaning equipment used aboard all tankers (including of course *Rania Chandris*) the industry had seen, just four years previously, a number of explosions that had hit three VLCCs: the *Matra, Marpessa* and *King Hakkon IV* within the space of a few weeks. One of the ships sank, while the other two suffered considerable damage and loss of life and injury to crew. As all three tankers were tank cleaning at the time of the explosions, IMO crude oil tanker specialists worked extremely quickly to investigate further the possibility that during this operation they might find the cause. It was concluded that a spark from the tank-cleaning machines had met the highly inflammable mixture of oxygen and hydrochloride gases that were swirling around the tank at sufficient levels to create the explosions.

The history of this superb safety feature was chequered but interesting. As prime instigators, some major British and American oil companies, the Classification Societies (especially the Technical Association of Lloyd's Register), plus experts from the International Chamber of Shipping (ICS), the Oil Companies International forum (OCIMF), INTERTANKO, and of course IMCO, turned to the numerous tests begun as long ago as 1925. These investigations into ways of introducing a neutralising agent into crude oil cargo tanks were subsequently revised at the end of the Second World War.

The findings were re-energised following the VLCC explosions and led directly to universal adoption, under the MARPOL73/78 Protocols, directed initially at crude oil carriers in excess of 100,000sdwt. The assumption was that only ships in and above this category would use the very powerful tank-cleaning machines causing the problem. Eventually, the success of the venture deemed it appropriate for IGS to be extended to crude oil, chemical and liquid gas tankers of all but the smallest capacity classes.

Above left: *The resulting extent of an explosion on board the VLCC* King Hakkon IV *caused by a spark from a cleaning machine igniting highly inflammable hydrochloride gas within the cargo tank. The introduction of oxygen-free inert flue gases taken from the ship's boilers, cleaned and channelled through the cargo tanks, eliminated this type of horrific accident. (Martin Leduc/seafarermedia.com)*

Above right and below: *Damage to main deck and tank caused by explosions during tank-cleaning operations on board a second VLCC. (Both Dennis Cleaver of Durban, South Africa)*

The success of the experiments was based firmly on physics, mindful that an explosion can only occur if there is combustible material, oxygen and a source of ignition. The solution (remaining in use today) found ways of eliminating oxygen as the easiest to deal with of the three and was achieved by using flue gases from the tanker's boilers, remaining after the oxygen had been used to fire the main engine. This hot mixture of carbon monoxide and nitrogen plus a few other flue gas mixtures, together with water and various solid particles including soot, was initially pumped through a scrubber tower. Here, it was washed with water drawn from sea water intakes, before being pumped through a demister, after which the refined gas was blown into pipe lines leading across the main deck into all cargo tanks. A deck seal was used to prevent any possible reversal of flow of hydrocarbon gas back into the engine room machinery spaces. The air from the tanks was eventually expelled by powerful fans via a purge pipe or a high-velocity pressure vacuum valve fitted to a suitable mast. The success of this maritime venture was profound, for there have subsequently been no recorded accidents to tankers fitted with IGS from this cause, where the system has been used correctly.

A further offshoot of IGS was the elimination of the high-velocity ventilation valves used to serve each tank. Additional gear included permanently fixed tank-cleaning machines, invariably fitted at the bottom of the tanks.

In the wheelhouse and chart areas we were blessed with a new device: a massive box-like object that we were informed was a computer designed to help achieve more efficiently the aims of navigation aboard ships of all classes, to find the way, avoid collision, and maintain a schedule. Computers had appeared at sea in elementary forms since the 1960s and, inevitably, had improved as more sophisticated devices appeared on the market. The engineering department probably lent itself best to computerisation, and already much discussion was taking place, hinting at the future existence of a fully automatic engine room. This indeed occurred within a few years.

Navigators continued to use traditional methods to achieve these first aims, but already methods were being closely examined by technologists to use new satellite systems for position fixing. As mentioned, aboard *Rania Chandris* we were already the grateful possessors of computerised radar, which made a major contribution towards anti-collision assessments and warnings when a selected target vessel came within a stipulated distance from our own ship. This obviated the previous manual plotting that, reducing a distance of 12 miles or so to a 2ft radius diagram, was time-consuming and largely inaccurate especially when – alone on the bridge – the officer of the watch may have been dealing with more than one target ship. We were pleased to note that we now had a later model that did the same job, but much quicker with a clearer display. Hints were already being made about fully integrated satellite-based communications systems, news that was obviously ill-received by the world's posse of radio officers. This also happened within a few years.

Maintaining the voyage plan of a vessel had increased considerably in importance with the advent of ships as large as V/ULCCs – and for colleagues serving aboard the new container ships that were rapidly appearing to replace three or four average-sized, deep-sea, dry-cargo ships. Both the master and chief engineer both made me only too well aware of the importance of paying close attention to my duties in this direction. It seemed that our ship cost around £18 per minute to run, which was to the order of £2,400 per day or £0.8 million per year, which, as Captain Agnew pointed out, was 'one hell of a lot of Mars bars!' Clearly, the shipping industry *per se* was being forced to renounce firmly the old 'hit and miss, by guess and by God' methods of navigation of preceding years.

The ideal speed at which any VLCC closed its jetty was plus/minus 3ft per minute with a yaw or swinging of the bow at an angular momentum of 0.05 degrees/minute. These minute distances had always proved difficult to assess by human senses and were normally 'guesstimated' (with fairly reasonable degrees of accuracy) by the experience attained over the years by various masters and pilots. Two displays indicated the velocity port/starboard fore and aft, and the yaw at the bow and stern as well as an indication of our true ground track. So we greeted our new-fangled

Doppler radar with interest. We were, it seemed, given this device in preference to an alternative Doppler that worked on sound assessments.

I had followed these novel introductions with professional interest and eagerly looked forward to taking a short-duration Electronic Navigational Aids certificate updating course at my nearest School of Navigation in the Minories, London, as soon as this could be fitted into a leave.

★ ★ ★

I grabbed the opportunity of going into the dry dock with Paul and extending my knowledge of the duties he had performed in preparation and during this operation. He admitted his gratitude for help received from the relief chief and second officers that opened his eyes to things he would never have expected might fall into this new role. In turn, I also learnt what might be expected of me undoubtedly at some future date aboard either this or another VLCC when it fell to my turn to supervise a dry-docking of these monsters. Even so, it was a strange sensation walking underneath *Rania Chandris* aware of 320,000 tons of light deadweight ship resting above me!

It was only a few days after we had re-joined that welcome instructions were received for officers to leave their hotel and the crew to depart from their lodgings, repair on board while the dry dock was flooded, and then with pilot and tugs happily in place, sail for our long-deferred third voyage.

Slipping into the second mate role was comparatively pain free and straightforward. I had, of course, been well acquainted with these duties aboard dry-cargo ships and was sufficiently experienced on VLCCs for there to be few problems in transition but, nevertheless, similar to the first of my two voyages during my initial tour as third officer on the *Rania Chandris*, I was left largely to my own devices by senior officers to slot into new duties as her second officer. This was helped by me being totally relaxed and with complete peace of mind. On the short train trip from my home in south-east London, the previous lingering doubts that had assailed my mind when I joined such a large tanker for my first voyage were totally dispelled. For on this re-joining, I knew what I was going back to. I knew

Under-keel shot of the 190,000-ton VLCC Myrina *in dry dock prior to launching showing the packing, keel and bilge supports. It was a strange sensation standing underneath my own supertanker only too aware of the enormous mass of vessel above me. (Shell Tankers)*

Left and below: *During a dry-docking the anchor cable is laid out completely along the dock floor while the opportunity is taken not only to clean the enormous links, but to look for any cracks that might have appeared, due as much to metal fatigue as anything else. (Both A. McEwan, Mobil Shipping)*

the majority of fellow officers with whom I would sail. An excellent relationship had been forged with Captain Agnew and Derek, my immediate
seniors, who I knew were all too willing to help me where this might be
asked for. And, equally as importantly, complete familiarity was felt with
most of my duties that were associated with this undoubted monster of a
ship. Of course, there remained much to learn regarding cargo handling,
but I knew also these new duties could be assimilated.

In turn, it was good to help Charles as requested, and his assistance
was welcomed with the taking of morning sights and remaining for the
noon position fix. This latter procedure was the maritime equivalent of
Communion Service in a High Anglican cathedral, evoking memories of
long past distant cathedral chorister days. Often Captain Agnew popped
up with his trusty gun to join us and, democratically, allowed his position
to be intermingled with ours to form an average that was taken as gospel.

Associated with this new task now was my daily liaison with the chief
engineer to compare my observed position and speed with that attained
by the ship's engines. Invariably, this proved a moment of some hilarity
because the two positions of where the ship could be never tallied completely. Any chief aboard any ship in the world's merchant navies worth
his salt swore blind to O'Reilly (whoever this mythical character might
be) that the engines of his ship always arrived in port days ahead of the
remainder of the vessel. So, the ceremony was always conducted with
great solemnity and some tongue-in-cheek humour, with the difference
attributed to that delightful nautical euphemism termed 'slip per cent'.

Recommencing the second officer's traditional watch-keeping roles of
taking the 12 to 4 morning and afternoon watches was strange but easily
overcome, along with the inevitable chart and nautical publications cor-
recting. As we were both new to our positions, Derek discussed any query
areas that came my way, while I introduced Charles to his new delights. I
had to say it was with no regrets that I relinquished my LSA duties, including servicing and maintaining the open lifeboats. It was time to move on.

A further duty easily imbibed was being directly responsible to Captain
Agnew for voyage planning. After discussing with him distances off shore

The daily ritual when the second officer brought his offering to the chief engineer of the ship's noon position was invariably one of some hilarity. The observed position invariably varied from the theoretical position of the tanker deduced from the twenty-four-hour run of the engines. The compared difference was referred to as 'the day's slip per cent'. (BP plc)

Any new second officer found it useful to discuss with and gain a second opinion from his immediate superior, the chief officer, regarding potential query areas. (BP plc)

from major waypoints on the voyage, I now spent more time in the chart area preparing voyage plans based on this information, and taking into account other factors such as area zones, weather forecasts and tidal information, before making my final decision and discussing this with the captain. My courses and distances were then run off on small-scale charts and afterwards transferred to the in-use large-scale charts. Also, charts were ordered and the various folios covering areas of the world's oceans where our ship would be likely to travel kept up to date. Inevitably, appropriate Admiralty pilots for these areas were requested, and those books to which the ship would never be called, such as the Black Sea, could be used as temporary props wedging our automatic steering pilot to the forward bulkhead. This move helped ease problems caused by the excessive vibration continuing to bedevil our steering!

In my new capacity, I set the scene admirably with Captain Agnew when offering him my first voyage plan by advising that, 'I have worked on the theory, Sir, that we shall be turning left at Land's End.' The emotions crossing his face were my just reward, making any verbal comment superfluous, apart from what sounded like an adenoidal grunt! I suppose it showed that I was at least relaxed in approaching my duties.

The next difference arising from my promotion was automatically taking charge aft for berthing and departure stations. I had been well prepared for this over previous trips through Captain Agnew's admirable training policy, but was now a direct party involved in the berthing planning, discussing with master and pilot the sequence for running out the moorings and where the taking of tugs was required, and which ones would be only in attendance and not made fast. Variable tidal conditions for some berthing operations, for example, meant the plan called for warps sometimes to constitute a mixture of polypropylene ropes and wires, or for all wires to be used.

An additional new duty assigned to me was running the ship's sickbay. All deck officers, even in those early VLCC days, were required to follow a basic First Aid certificate course ashore run usually by the British Red Cross or St John's Ambulance Brigade. All seafarers, before joining any Red Ensign ship, invariably underwent a medical examination but were

Every week, senior officers met in the captain's cabin or office to discuss professional aspects arising before and during the voyage. Occasionally, other officers were invited to attend to offer their specific areas of specialisation. (BP plc)

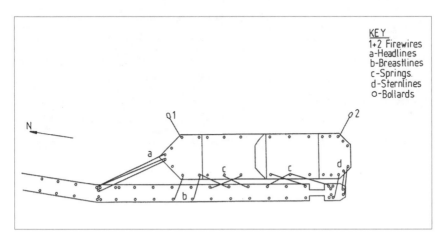

KEY
1+2 Firewires
a-Headlines
b-Breastlines
c-Springs.
d-Sternlines
o-Bollards

A mooring plan for a VLCC at a jetty set in a strong tidal flow necessitated the doubling up of back springs, helping to keep this very large ship firmly alongside.

a pretty healthy lot, generally speaking. The requirements usually covered attending to simple accidents or minor sickness that, with crews of all nationalities, often included a disinclination to work more than anything more serious! This was treated with initially a gentle 'tea and sympathy' approach, or with the seasoned campaigner the threat of a good dose of black draught laxative. For more serious injuries, such as a man having an

Above and opposite: *The exercise of the correct use of compressed air breathing apparatus was an essential drill aboard tankers. Not that this happened frequently, but I recall one real emergency aboard a dry-cargo ship that occurred when a man was overcome by paint fumes while working in a tank and it became essential to enter the enclosed compartment to rescue him. He then required the administering of oxygen to help his recovery. As the ship's 'medical officer', I kept a close eye on him for a day or so, but fortunately he seemed to suffer no visible serious ill effects and was soon able to pop back to work. (Both BP plc)*

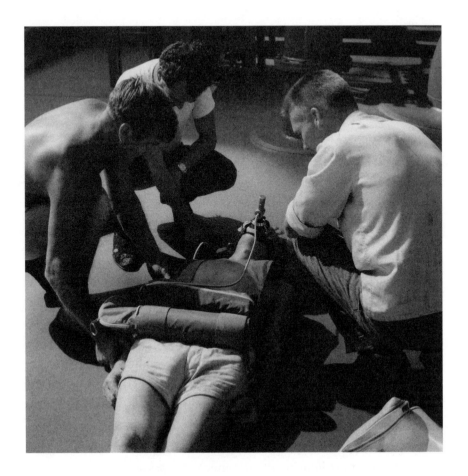

accident slipping on deck and not wearing his safety helmet, the resulting concussion was referred to the master, with the option of contacting a shore station or any Royal naval vessel or liner carrying in her complement a qualified ship's surgeon. We invariably had the option when in range of lifting a man to shore-side hospital by helicopter, although I never knew of any incidents where this became necessary.

Our weekly fire and boat station emergency drills remained as conscientious as ever. These did not vary from the two previous trips. I was assigned to Derek's number two lifeboat, but continued to alternate with Charles and Tim following boat drills leading a party on either fire hose/

foam-water monitors, stretcher and rescue, or rigging my crew in breathing apparatus and resuscitating equipment.

Nearly two months later, as we cleared the African coast off Socotra, Derek succumbed to my requests by giving a brief introduction to cargo loading. He had just received and discussed with the master our orders from the owners. The radio message had advised the quantity of our cargo expressed in the conventional measurements of barrels, based on a standard measurement of net barrels or the volume that our cargo would occupy at the traditional base temperature of 60°F. He then had to recalculate this into deadweight tonnage at the appropriate Plimsoll load line commensurate with the areas and seasons likely to be encountered during our passage.

It seemed on this third voyage we were to load at Ras Tanura 50,000 tons Arabian Heavy and 213,000 tons Light for discharge as follows: at Sète in the Gulf of Lyons we would make fast to a single-buoy mooring (SBM) and discharge the 50,000 tons of Heavy from numbers one and four centre tanks, plus 50,000 tons Light. We would then procced on passage to Wilhelmshaven, who would take 40,000 Light, with the balance going to my favourite jetty at Coryton. It seemed the mooring off Sète required a maximum draft of 69ft or around 270,000 tons deadweight, which clearly had to be considered in terms of loading, plus expenditure of heavy fuel, diesel and lubricating oils, as well as cabin stores, etc, consumed during the seventeen-day passage.

Derek then introduced his brand-new 'toy', a loading computer, and offered an insight into the necessity of this in assessing what were known technically as bending moments and shear stresses on the hull, or limits of hogging and sagging. Which of these latter would be involved was dependent upon whether or not the tanker was loaded, respectively, with more weight at the ends of the hull than in the middle.

Making the correct assessments of these longitudinal stresses was a vitally important consideration. The average supertanker is not built like a girder with weight distributed equally along its length, and when in light displacement mode or unladen prior to ballasting, most of the weight acts at the after end owing to the position of the engines and the accommodation block. In this state she would sit literally on top of the water. The bottom of the bulbous bow and entire length are exposed towards the mid-part of number one tank, when there is a gradual submerging along the bottom of the hull until an after draught of just a few feet is reached such that both propeller and rudder are only partially submerged. Thus a series of longitudinal stresses are caused, creating an imbalance of forces along the hull, with resultant stresses acting upon the ship's frames. These are called 'shearing forces', hence 'bending moments' because they tend to distort the hull to its breaking or shearing point. They act locally through the corners of the tanks. During the loading (and of course discharging) of the ship, therefore, these forces have to be kept within safe limits. One has to be mindful of stresses likely to be incurred throughout the entire voyage. It is impossible to load any VLCC without creating stresses. If these cause a tendency for the ends of the ship to lift, with the middle part dropping, the condition is known as 'hogging' and, if the ends lift with the centre dropping, it is called 'sagging'. The possibility of either of these conditions occurring are assessed within safe limits and then built into the construction of the ship. It is quite common and perfectly safe in any kind of rough seaway to see the main deck moving slightly, which accounts for the expansion joints fitted into some of the pipes extending the length of the vessel.

There are also a series of transversal stresses that have to be taken into consideration concurrently that affect any possible port or starboard listing of the vessel. When working out these stress loads on the ship, therefore, two centres have to be considered: the weight of the ship acting through its centre of gravity, and the up-thrust of the water acting through her centre of buoyancy. Aboard smaller tankers, paper tables, such as those produced by the firm Tunnard, are used with perfect safety, but the magnitude of forces requiring accurate assessment aboard larger tankers are too complex, hence the need for computerisation.

Armed with this information, the number of operations in which I had participated on my previous two voyages suddenly gained additional clarity. I appreciated more fully the reasons why we had transferred ballast between tanks while the ship was under way. This had to happen to take

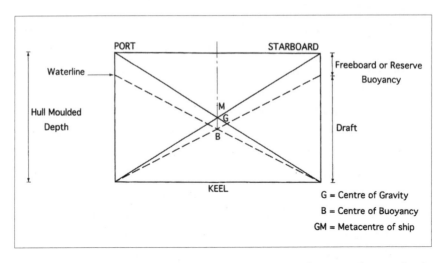

A diagram indicating theories contained in assessing transversal stresses. These involve the metacentre (M) of a ship, which is the point around which any transversal moment will occur between the centres of gravity (G) and buoyancy (B). The complexities involved in assessing longitudinal stresses require use of a loading computer, which also automatically takes transversal stresses into consideration.

The chief officer aboard a large VLCC uses a Loadmaster stress indicator, likely to result in the vicinity of numbers one and two cargo tanks using predetermined test calculations. Dials on the extreme right display the trim and draught of the ship. On this particular supertanker, the permissible trim errors were 10in when she was loaded, and 21in when in ballast. (BP plc)

Above left: *The pump control panel aboard BP's* British Explorer *displaying the condition of the pumps, speed and discharge pressures. (BP plc)*

Above right: *Cargo and ballast valve control panel on a large 1970s VLCC. (BP plc)*

into account the consumption of fuel and stores. In the process of learning, greater appreciation of the numerous tank valve and pump controls in the cargo control room was imbibed.

★ ★ ★

Loading at Ras Tanura proceeded without any delays or hitches, and our passage to the Frontignam SBM serving the oil port at Sète opposite Marseilles was without incident. Another first for me was taking the mooring buoy. We entered the dredged channel and began the 5.2-mile approach in fresh east-south-east force 8 to 9 winds. As it was far too rough to take the buoy, we anchored for a day or so until conditions had moderated considerably, before taking the pilot. The vessel was then turned at dead slow ahead to pick up the floating mooring lines provided at the buoy.

SBMs are substantially constructed and fixed firmly to the seabed with a combination of sinker and grapnel-type anchors whose mushroom shape digs firmly into the mud. The buoys are so constructed that they allow

A modern VLCC lying quietly to a single-buoy mooring (SBM) showing the connections between manifolds and buoy. (BP plc)

the ship to swing to any condition of tide. The oil pipelines are flexible and float on top of the sea. They are picked up by a launch and connected over the bows of the tanker to run through a specially constructed stopper that is held more firmly to the buoy. A submerged cargo pipeline, through which the oil can be discharged using the ship's pumps, runs through the centre of the buoy and leads to the refinery. Our discharge of the two grades took about sixteen hours. As a sign of my now 'tanker maturity', as Derek (inevitably) described the condition, I was left on my own to complete the discharge from both number three wing tanks.

We had departed Sète SBM and settled on course for Cape de Creus when the master came to the bridge advising that the engine room had notified him that the inner seal in the lubricating oil used for cooling purposes in the propeller shaft stern tube was leaking at the rate of 5 gallons per minute. He emphasised how serious a defect this could prove as the problem could only be fixed by shore technicians using specially adapted tools. He stated that there were none available in France, although the Lindo Yard had stated it could fly out a technician to Marseilles in 'about three days' time'. More immediately, so far as I was concerned, we would have to turn the ship through 180 degrees and return to Sète anchorage. We had already reduced the engine proportionately to 23rpm, so I was left to turn the ship onto a reciprocal course. The distance to the fairway buoy was 55 miles and I started to turn the ship at 0123 hrs. Initially, she came round very quickly but, as the momentum of the vast beam kicked in, the remainder of her turn was extremely sluggish. It was only after thirty-five minutes that I was able to steady the ship onto 015 degrees (T) and start the laborious return trip.

This journey was bedevilled by a large fleet of fishing boats, many of whom cut directly across our bows and totally disregarding our Not Under Command (NUC) signals. Being something of a more hardened campaigner nowadays, I simply ignored them, leaving each to its own devices. In such a cavalier fashion we finally crawled back to Sète sometime during Tim's watch.

As I lay in my bunk drinking my early morning tea, I did not need the steward to inform me that we were once more under way. Popping into the saloon for breakfast next day, Derek informed me that the engineers had made a slight misjudgement in their original diagnosis. On opening the patient, they discovered that the seal had not broken as previously thought, but had merely become dislodged. This had been reset and the patient stitched up, so the vessel set off on her voyage once more as cables were despatched to the owners and Lindo yard telling them the good news and cancelling all further arrangements. Needless to say, my next chess venture with the third engineer was a time for more 'gentle leg-pulling', although he had his revenge by winning both games.

Regular chats with Captain Agnew were by now the norm. Although remaining deeply respectful of him and his profound specialist knowledge, the little imp that had so bedevilled my childhood days that had got me into (and often out of) numerous incidents, remained just below the surface. It surfaced now and again in gentle teasing. I found, for example, that any favourable mention of the Labour Party was extremely effective: he would quietly bristle and then, were I to defend any specific point, become (for him) slightly more agitated. Of course, after a few incidents the realisation came that I was (perhaps) being something of a devil's advocate: 'Oh my goodness, Mr Solly, I do believe you are winding me up!'

'Oh come now, Sir. Would I do such a dastardly thing as that?'

After that would emanate his gentle smile and deep chuckle that, in my memory banks, I continue associating with this first-class man.

As we cleared the Bay of Biscay in storm-force stern winds, heavy seas and swell, with visibility fogged by rain-laden cloud, he dropped his bombshell. I had just altered course to starboard for yet another recalcitrant trawler performing its customary gymnastics a mile or so dead ahead. He waited until *Rania Chandris* was settled back onto as near her course line as possible in the atrocious weather conditions when he announced his intention of retiring at the end of the voyage. 'You know, Mr Solly, I have been at sea continuously since I was 16 years of age, and even longer if you take into account three years at Pangbourne. I just feel I have had enough and should like to spend more time at home with my wife and family. And even, who knows, seeing something more of my own country for a change.'

'Oh, I am sorry to hear that, Sir. I really hope everything works out well for you.'

We left the conversation at that while busying ourselves with our various customary shipboard duties, but I have to say thoughts remained tickling my mind. I had become very used to his ways, and indeed his consideration to all others. Yes, he could (rightfully) be strict when this proved necessary, but generally once his standards had been accepted by his officers, he was indeed a gentleman – and a damn good captain under whom to serve. I certainly placed him top of the listing of my five best master mariners I encountered while at sea.

★ ★ ★

One of those euphemistic 'errors of judgement' was made in the English Channel shortly after we had cleared Les Casquets light on passage to Wilhelmshaven. I wandered up to the wheelhouse to complete some of the ubiquitous corrections to charts and navigational publications and casually noticed a small coaster about 10 degrees off our starboard bow. To this initial cursory glance, she seemed rather too close for comfort. On passing the chart table into the wheelhouse to make an encouraging mug of coffee, I noticed Charles concentrating intensely on settings of the Decca Navigator. Suddenly, his agitated secunny rushed into the wheelhouse shouting to the world at large: 'Ah Sahib, ship starboard now make closer.' Charles immediately left the Decca and raced around to the steering console: knocked 'Mad Mike' into manual and shoved the wheel hard a starboard. I joined him at the wheelhouse front, watching our bows as dramatically slowly they cleared the ship with a mean margin of safety. As we passed the thing down our port side, I noticed the bridge on the coaster was completely devoid of personnel: no one was on watch! The crew there had no idea how closely they had come to meeting a watery grave. With shaking hands (oh how I knew that feeling), Charles explained he had thought atmospheric conditions were suitable for changing the Decca Navigator lanes so, with the reported coaster 10 miles ahead, had concentrated on his task, completely forgetting all about the other ship. At that moment, Captain Agnew came onto the bridge from the starboard ladder and, giving the third a very direct look, enquired what might be happening on board his ship. As tactfully as the situation allowed, I popped back behind the curtain and busied myself with my corrections …

I was called from my corrections by Captain Agnew telling me he had just received a cable from 'the Kremlin' advising our port of discharge was now Europoort once more and not Germany, so 'could I kindly readjust the charts and prepare for the deep-water anchorage'. But as we closed this, he returned and, smiling widely, informed me our orders had again been changed, for we were now to go alongside immediately and take the pilots who were already heading for our vessel. Being well accustomed to the vagrancies of supertanker trading by now, I merely nodded agreement and placed my tindal, or next senior rating to the serang, on standby with his lads and then popped aft for an uneventful but lengthy operation bringing the ship alongside.

BP's magnificent VLCC British Respect *was built in 1974 and was the flagship of the company's fleet. Her beam of 55.25m made an impressive sight. (BP plc)*

The British Norness *is seen departing her berth at the company's Grain refinery in Kent, taking just two tugs to assist her safely to leave the berth. It was quite common for navigators to form an affinity with another vessel. We were being overtaken on passage towards Cape Town by this magnificent 260,950sdwt supertanker, which was marginally faster than* Rania Chandris. *Over the ensuing ten days, we made regular VHF contact, exchanging news and views about our respective companies, conditions of service, progressing to family details and other sundry matters. (BP plc)*

Another 'new' development for me occurred as we came alongside Coryton. I was well advanced with supervising the crew in preparing my moorings when Derek suddenly appeared on the after deck. He told me he was taking over as the master wanted an accurate visual draught of the vessel and I was to board the attendant Port of London Authority's launch, whose boarding and berthing inspector had kindly agreed to assist. I immediately popped down the gangway and, taking my trusty work notebook from the breast pocket of my boiler suit, took the required draught. As we passed ahead of the slow-moving supertanker, the full width of these monster ships was really brought home to me in this unexpected way. By now my stock of superlatives had run well dry, so I just looked and admired. But actually seeing from this unusual navigator's view the width of these monster tankers reinforced the reason why making that 180-degree turn off Sète had taken such a long time.

I did my ordinary cargo watches once alongside, discharging numbers one to four wing tanks, but was told by Derek that I could go home for a long weekend, if I wished, for local leave. This was totally unexpected, but I did not waste any time: a taxi was quickly called for a direct ship-to-home run, where the unexpected holiday was well spent and enjoyed. Coming back on board was an easy matter. I took the train to Gravesend and then picked up a pilot boat heading for a tanker anchored in the Nore. This kindly dropped me off at Coryton. The long climb up the vertical jetty ladder was worthwhile, but the concern immediate on my mind was to find out who had replaced Captain Agnew as master. Derek simply smiled and stated: 'Ah, so you too have fallen for the Old Man's equally as old chestnut, have you?'

It appeared that he was indeed still on board and, although it had not been mentioned, other regular officers serving with him had been regaled with the same retirement story. I did cast him a 'more than direct' look when reporting to him that I was back on board, but received only one of his famous whimsical smiles in return! Within minutes of being back on board, I had changed into the deck officer's 'uniform' of boiler suit and white hard hat, and was on cargo watch relieving Charles until lunchtime.

It became something of a routine on subsequent trips for the master to make the same announcement roughly at the same point on the passage in the same serious tones until, eventually, I told him, 'Do you know, Sir, I have heard *some* mention of this before on previous trips, but I think the only way you will ever leave this ship will either be when it is laid up, or when they carry you down the gangway and along the jetty in your box!'

This proved a comment that, to give him his due, he met with an open chuckle, an engaging grin, and a rueful head shaken in agreement.

A further perennial voyage topic was the frequency of house moves that he planned for each leave, most of which were instituted by his restless wife. He had married late in life, and while undoubtedly master of his own ship, I was not so sure this was reflected when he was at home. Certainly, on the one occasion when she visited the ship, imperiously demanding tones could be heard emanating from the master's day room, calling him by name, and dragging him away from a quiet beer with the chief officer. He responded to these 'royal commands' with all the alacrity of a junior cadet being called by his captain: a source of considerable secret amusement between us all!

Before we sailed, Derek introduced me to the ballasting operation in the cargo control room, opening a few more tricks of my still comparatively new trade. But, within a day or so, we were under way, completing the final voyage of my second tour.

A number of topics of professional conversation invariably arose while taking coffee in the smoke room after lunch intermingled with the social and casual chat. On one occasion, a comment between the master and chief engineer fell into the general pool that discussed the potential of double-hulled VLCCs. This arose from a number of associated topics, not least an incident of oil spillage that had been reported in that bastion of shipping news, *Lloyd's List*. It brought into play other factors such as stability, with enhanced hull strengthening resulting from a possible five longitudinal bulkheads, and perhaps the double sides being used for ballast water. A number of other 'possibilities' became bandied around, but in the end conversation lapsed after we had produced a collective

Rania Chandris *with cargo discharged, correctly ballasted and ready for sea. At 286,000sdwt, she was then the largest vessel to go alongside Coryton and one of the biggest in deadweight capacity to enter the Port of London's jurisdiction. Walking on deck to take charge aft, and occasionally up forward on later trips, never occasioned a sense of familiarity, but always a feeling of responsibility; aware that constant vigilance was essential to avoid accidents. (Port of London Authority)*

master VLCC approaching well beyond the bounds of credibility, let alone probability!

What was not so impossible was the forecast of increasing computerisation across all departments. Here, of course, deck–engine rivalry reared again its awesome head as the strong probability of a theoretically unmanned engine room was raised. The implications of this led to much tongue-in-cheek humour that was brought to a halt when temperatures in the engine room, as it were, started to rise a little.

★ ★ ★

I served a further two tours of duty aboard *Rania Chandris*, each of the promised two months' duration covering the 22,000-mile return journey between the Gulf oilfields, including Mina al Ahmadi, Kharg Island and Ras Tanura before discharging generally at Europoort before heading for Coryton. There were many officer changes during this period, but core senior officers and engineers seemed happy to remain with the ship.

Inevitably, numerous and varied situations arose during these trips built around the stability of a consistently regular run with officers among whom a degree of familiarity existed. Although most officers who joined us were of sound quality, a few fell below the company's (and our own) traditional standards. Alcohol was the major cause leading them eventually to 'walk the proverbial plank' at the earliest opportunity. A third officer and then a junior engineer soon proved to be rampaging drunkards. The former was completely intoxicated when I relieved the watch at midnight. He had seemingly spent the watch sitting on the settee, used as a dumping ground for an assortment of gear, with his head in his hands while we were still crossing the Bay of Biscay. He clearly did not know whether he was on board a supertanker or the *Royal Scot*. I glanced at his quartermaster, who was chatting to his relief. Both looked at me despairingly and simply raised their eyes heavenwards. It was pointless discussing things with them, but I mentioned the incident to Derek the next day and he clearly passed this on to Captain Agnew, who asked me point blank what had happened. The third was clearly incapable of doing his job and was a menace to us, to himself, and to other shipping. On learning the facts, Captain Agnew sent for the third and he was another soon on his way, along with subsequently the junior engineer.

It was the number of collisions and dangerous incidents arising from such widespread abuse of alcohol among watch keepers, combined with an abundance of unqualified deck and engineering officers recruited internationally among shipping companies of all nationalities, that led (inevitably) to maritime organisations ashore expressing justifiable alarm.

Inevitably, the driving forces resulting in action were the international marine insurance companies, who were left to pick up the tab of these disasters. It would, however, be a further twenty years before international standards for all watch keepers serving aboard any of the world's merchant ships became formulated, agreed, introduced and enforced by regulations and protocols that were backed by IMO.

Many of these events were already in their infant stages. For example, we were now as a matter of course holding boat drills with all officers and ratings dressed appropriately in protective clothing and hard hats. Computerisation had gained slight momentum in all departments. Even, horror upon horror to sparkys internationally, discussions covered rumours heard from various professional sources ashore about new-fangled 'satellite navigation and communication systems' threatening to replace the world's navy of radio officers. It did not take the appearance of a 'nautical Delphic Oracle' with palm either crossed or not crossed with silver to determine that the future of merchant seafaring seemed lined up for a considerable shake-up that would alter the *modus* out of all proportion to what we serving in the 1970s could either imagine or even suspect.

★ ★ ★

A significant event occurred on a subsequent trip when I was duty officer. This duty was more common on dry-cargo ships, which rarely worked cargo overnight, so it occurred on *Rania Chandris* during my time aboard only on two or three occasions. The duty was shared between us three mates below chief officer and was hardly onerous; it meant merely being on standby and notifying the duty quartermaster where he could be found. Strictly functional, the officer remained asleep in his cabin until woken by the officer's steward with a welcome tray of tea.

On duty at Tranmere in the port of Liverpool on a rare occasion when we deviated from Coryton, I was given a very rude awakening. The time was just after 0300 hrs when a frantic stomping and a frenetic banging on my door rudely awoke me from a deep sleep. This was accompanied by the sharp voice of my secunny urging me: 'Come quickly, Sahib, there is plenty atrouble.' I almost fell out of my bunk, and grabbing my boiler suit, the immediate item of clothing on hand, yanked this on and opened the door. In highly agitated breathless tones he explained: 'One of the Ag wallahs, Sahib, has made him adead – him a hanging in the crew washroom.'

Needless to say, all deck officers, including the master, had also been awakened. In fact, Captain Agnew was outside my door while I was calming the quartermaster. The captain suggested only the two of us accompanied the secunny to the washroom to see what had happened. The master told Derek to call the chief engineer, one deck below us, and then both should come to the ablutions.

The secunny told us as we went towards the engine room crew heads that one of the engine room ratings responding to a nightly call of nature had, to his shock and horror, discovered his colleague swinging from one of the shower heads. The ensuing commotion had, not surprisingly, roused the entire deck and engine room ratings, attracting the attention of the duty quartermaster from the gangway, leading him to race to my cabin. The master released the QM to return to the gangway while we entered the washroom.

The sight meeting our eyes has remained with me ever since. Doubtless it will still be with me when I make the same journey, but hopefully under more peaceful circumstances. The strangely lifeless body was hanging limply and forlornly, and had to be seen and treated in as detached a way as I could muster. It was the first time I had seen a man hanging and it was necessary as an act of will to submerge my instantly curious compassion, and force myself to look dispassionately at the gruesome sight confronting me. I noticed the smell first. He had clearly messed himself at some stage in the proceedings, and I immediately felt repulsion superseding my original charitable thoughts.

We had to act, so Captain Agnew, also clearly shaken but very much in at least outward control of his thoughts and feelings, and indeed the situation, told me to support the weight of the body while he would cut him down with the penknife all deck officers accustomed to cargo ships invariably carry in their pockets somewhere. It was only by exercising considerable will power that I could force myself to place my arms round the trunk of that still warm and stinking corpse in an act of disturbed and almost disgusted love. The master used my jackknife to saw through the cord supporting him. Perhaps as a revelation of his own emotions and in an effort to lighten our actions, he muttered casually: 'Your knife needs sharpening, Mr Solly.' We laid the man gently in the scuppers.

By this time the chief officer and engineer had arrived. I was told by the captain to go to the ship's office and notify the local police, explaining what had happened and asking them to call a doctor and ambulance.

I was not sorry to leave the scene of this appalling horror, alive with recollections of what I had just done, and the sadness in the situation that had caused the wiper to commit such a terribly tragic act. I could still smell and feel the body, replaying in my mind the repulsive actions I had been forced to take, and the equally sickening scenes I had been forced to witness. I found that compassion had indeed been driven into a secret recess of my mind by the circumstances of the situation.

Certainly, no answers could be found despite my struggles, but I was left with plenty of questions. My secunny asked me with a doleful expression, 'Why this man ado this thing, Sahib? For what reason he act this way?' There was nothing I could say or do to reassure him, except explain gently that I quite simply did not know, so could not answer his questions. The same train of thought had clearly affected us both.

My reverie was broken by the silent arrival of the police in the form of a uniformed sergeant and constable, whom I instructed my quartermaster to take below. While awaiting the ambulance and police doctor's car, I was joined by Derek and we chatted quietly. Again the same questions were bandied around, but he also enquired how I was thinking about and reacting to things. Although appreciating his concern for me, there was little I could share. Physical sickness lurked not far below the surface of my sensitivity and even drinking a glass of water seemed repugnant.

As soon as the doctor arrived, Derek took him below, by which time my secunny had returned. I told him to wait for the ambulance and then show them below while I went to see how things were faring. The police sergeant was in full concentrated mode, with his constable taking careful notes. Captain Agnew mentioned there was little for me to do, but I should go and wait in my cabin until I heard him returning to his day room, when I should join them.

In need of some kind of company, I joined the other officers in the smoke room, but the conversations there were far from comforting and I silently slid away to my cabin. My immediate concern was to shower. I threw my revolting boiler suit and underclothes into a corner of the shower cubicle, meaning to wash these later in the day. I could not possibly allow my Goanese officer's steward to touch these repulsive rags that were bearing stains and smells that would not bear too close examination. Five minutes after I had dressed into a clean uniform, Tim joined me and together we waited quietly, just mostly sharing each other's company, until I heard the lift stop, then the bustle of life herald the captain and his retinue. I joined the mate, police, chief and second engineers and the doctor just crammed into the study. As we passed into the master's day room, Derek told me that the ambulance had only just gone. It was then down to business with a welcome stiff brandy easing the proceedings.

The situation was far from normal for we were now a Liberian-registered ship with British crew and Asian ratings, but it was still necessary for the appropriate formal entries to be made in the official log book. These were then signed by the police sergeant, doctor, and senior ship's officers, while I was instructed to write a statement of events relating my involvement and pass this signed document to the master for inclusion in the log. Following another tot of brandy to act as a wake for the poor wiper, the police and doctor left. The former informed us that the coroner's office would be notified next day, leaving the ship to inform the Liberian embassy and Indian welfare officer (IWO). Ruefully perhaps, I mentioned to the master and Derek that the IWO would have something substantial on this occasion to justify his visit other than the petty and often imaged grievances that normally occupied his time. I made this remark without cynicism or rancour, for Asian crews aboard ships upon which I had worked blended extremely well with their officers. This enabled problems or even minor irritations to be ironed out at head of department and serang levels before these became concerns that required the intervention of even the Old Man, let alone the IWO. The engineers particularly were distressed to find out what had caused a member of their department to commit this tragic act, and even the most hardened junior was clearly shaken by the event. But no one, it appeared, could offer any constructive light regarding his motives.

By this time, I heard the breakfast gong so, actually being ready for a simple meal, popped into the saloon before going on deck for cargo watch. As officers and crew, we were far from our normal selves. Luckily, I had too much work to do to dwell on events, but lunch in the duty mess brought its own round of officers coming to terms with a suicide in their own ways. I was glad to leave, but on my way up to my cabin, the captain's tiger met me at the lift door to say the Master wanted me in his day room.

It seemed events had moved with lightning speed. In view of the ship sailing shortly, there was to be an inquest at 0900 hrs in Liverpool the next day and I was required to give evidence. Expressing my astonishment to Captain Agnew at British conservatism moving so swiftly, he simply smiled and I was then stood down until cargo watch in the evening.

When I returned to my cabin, I found my steward had already taken away my soiled clothing, washed and dried this and returned it ironed. I went and saw him where he was working in Tim's cabin, expressed my astonishment and thanked him quietly for what he had done. As a Goanese, his English was perfect, and making direct eye contact with me told me simply that this is what he had wanted to do for me. It was an act upon which he could not elaborate, but one that somehow would show his appreciation for what I had been forced to do in the dark hours of the night for a fellow rating, and that he understood something of what I was thinking and feeling. I backed off. I had already decided to ditch the clothes for I dreaded having to retouch them and place them into the promised bucket. The officer's steward and I reached a completely different level of understanding that I had never before experienced with a rating and would probably never again attain: we had both met the real person below the uniforms.

The inquest was little more than formality. The company provided a car to take the captain, chief engineer and me to attend a preliminary hearing of the coroner's court and give our evidence. It was certainly 'something different' for which to be relieved from my cargo watch. The police sergeant gave his evidence of finding the body after being called to the ship (which struck me as logical enough) and stated that he and his constable had not witnessed any circumstances that might have indicated foul play. I had not been aware they were even looking for anything of a criminal nature, but while listening ruefully, it suddenly dawned on me how different were our lifestyles and professional interests.

Inevitably, a little more of my inherent naivety disappeared down the plughole of life's experiences. Anyway, a preliminary verdict was returned of 'suicide whilst the balance of the mind was disturbed', which I supposed was as factually accurate as anything else, and served as an additional entry in the Old Man's official log book. It also served to satisfy (at least outwardly) the IWO and Liberian consul. But this verdict did not answer the question 'why'.

The next day we took on board our pilot and, with tugs fore and aft, headed out to Kharg Island for a full cargo of light and heavy crude. So gradually, as other events gained their own special momentum, shipboard life returned to normal. But I experienced a few disturbed nights' sleep for quite a long time.

★ ★ ★

We rarely carried deck or engineer cadets, but I recall one such 16-year-old first tripper who joined us as a deck cadet at the George. He had a pleasing personality and engaging smile that indicated professional promise. As Derek was engaged on a deep technical discussion with the master and chief engineer, it fell to my lot to welcome him to the hotel and show him his cabin. Chatting away amiably while he unpacked, I was a little perturbed to see a copy of the elementary book *Teach Yourself Navigation* fall out of his case! Gentle discussions over coffee informed me that he had attended the same Outward Bound Sea School at Aberdovey as I had, but while these schools were excellent in practical and 'character building' terms, in twenty-six days it was impossible to add any academic training. Any potential deck cadet needed something far more educationally substantial supporting his cadetship, otherwise he would be unlikely to cope with the rigorous demands of the second mates examination. As it would be my lot to take him for a two-hour morning session each week and set him academic exercises to do in his study, Derek and I began to feel some concern. Even before we joined the ship, his shortcomings gradually became apparent. He had passed no examinations at GCE (O) and had no knowledge of plane trigonometry, and he had studied general science and not the individual subjects of physics, chemistry and biology at school. Even more disturbing, he had not registered at nautical college for a second mate correspondence course. Anyway, we decided to see how he responded to professional academic tuition over the voyages, and make assessments of his ability to pass the first year Merchant Navy Training Board's (MNTB) syllabus.

Alas, by the time we reached Cape Town he was finding difficulty with simple arithmetic and algebraic equations. I told Derek and Captain Agnew that with hard work on his part I could have done something constructive with my side of his training, but his Saturday morning session with Derek revealed his inability to memorise correctly the most fundamental of collision regulations. At the end of his first voyage he had still not progressed beyond the first of the thirty-eight Collision Regulations, including four comprehensive Annexes. He was not, alas, 'the brightest knife in the drawer', as Derek (it just had to be) described the poor lad.

In a joint consultation between the three of us in Captain Agnew's day room, our suggestion that he terminate his cadetship was agreed. Derek discussed this with the boy, who admitted ruefully he would be sorry to give up his cadetship, but 'he had not realised the academic content of his training and could not see himself passing even the MNTB's annual exams, while second mate would be academically beyond him'. In the light of such an open admission, the captain passed these verdicts to Captain Branch, who apparently discussed this further with the boy's parents. We kept doing our best for him over the remainder of the complete tour of four months, but he finally left us with Captain Branch's promise that Chandris had consulted with the Shipping Federation who (very unusually, as we were a foreign flag vessel) had agreed to interview him with the view of offering a deck boy's berth with a UK company. He then passed out of our lives. But the memory of *Teach Yourself Navigation* has lived on.

$$\star \quad \star \quad \star$$

A number of further voyages were made on VLCCs before I left the Merchant Navy to enter academia, and then spend twenty years as a residential schoolmaster teaching in the complexly different world of two English independent schools. But, although blissfully unaware at the time, my tanker experiences were eventually to make a major contribution towards developing my third career, writing non-fiction books under commission and contract for traditional maritime markets.

On a purely personal level, memories continue to blend a kaleidoscope in my mind of strange pictures involving friendships, professionalism, and romanticism. Merely closing my eyes brings into focus sleek lines and an enormous funnel dwarfing five tiers of accommodation block, an image that has never lost its charm. I still 'see' broad expanses of foredeck from the wheelhouse windows with diminutive ant-like figures of the crew as they worked on deck. I recall much shared laughter with other officers. But equally as appreciated (even at the time) were clear unhindered views of passing horizons, making bridge watch-keeping such a delight, as *my* supertanker ploughed serenely through vast expanses of calmly untroubled azure seas.

But always, of course, images remain etched of 10,000grt ocean-going dry-cargo ships pitching and rolling wildly in typhoon- or hurricane-force winds and seas. For yes, I too have suffered aboard these vessels in such atrocious weather. But alas, human nature being what it undoubtedly is, I admit gentle humour in recalling their corkscrew antics from the stable platform of a 'maritime monster', appreciating soup that actually stayed in the dish – and a bowl that pleasingly remained on the table!

EPILOGUE

I came onto the scene roughly two-thirds of the way through a transitionary constructional period. Already, the world's insatiable demand for oil had led to ship owners of many nationalities deciding that owning such a vessel was a very lucrative business (which indeed it was!) This resulted in a glut of VLCC and ULCCs that was aided and abetted by a couple of Gulf Wars that led to many supertankers being scrapped with others used as storage hulks. These developments, in one sense, were not too disastrous. Those that fell under the breaker's tools were invariably of the older type that had caused many of the problems that have been encountered in this text, while the latter proved a gold mine for their owners. To fill a ship the size of *Jahre Viking* with crude oil, as indeed happened, and then to leave her safely anchored off a remote coast with a skeleton crew on board was prudent indeed: the value of her cargo over one year increased out of all proportion to the outlay! But the lifespan of all ULCCs exceeding 350,000 tons was limited and within a few years the entire fleet had been scrapped.

The size of the VLCC averaged out, by and large, to the ship of today around 300–320,000 tons. But alongside the demise in the number of these specialist ships from the mid to end of the 1970s was an increase in safety covering both the tanker and its environment. Some of these improvements had already been implemented by the time I transferred to VLCCs. In 1972, for instance, a new convention covering the international collision regulations had come into force replacing one that had served the industry since the 1860s.

As a by the by merely included for the sake of interest, the fact that Japan and north European countries (among others) gradually lost their holds over the tanker construction markets (as well as other classes of shipping) to South Korea is neither here nor there, except perhaps to the economies and workforces of these countries. Issues of safety are totally unaffected by where the ship is built because all vessels are covered by the same strictly enforced international regulations.

Today, as very much in the past, the general public are almost blissfully unaware of trends and developments in ship safety. IMO has for many years been very actively examining a range of relevant issues directly affecting all classes of the tanker trades.

The original MARPOL 73/78 regulations and protocols that came into force while I was still serving have been expanded beyond any recognition to levels that could not possibly have crossed my mind or that of those officers with whom I worked. The year 1976 saw the implementation by IMO of the convention that covered international marine satellites, known as INMARSAT. It was this agreement that would ultimately spelt the death knell for the carriage of radio officers.

In 1978, when I had already come ashore and was following university courses enabling me to qualify as a schoolmaster, the long-awaited and detailed IMO enquiries into the recruitment and certification of seafarers, making efforts to deal with the alcohol abuses, was instituted, although the ensuing convention would not become mandatory until the mid 1980s. An International Safety Management Code (ISM) followed in 1993. A Global Maritime Distress and Safety System (GMDSS) was set up in 1988 that would come into force only in 1992. The reason for such seemingly inordinate delays arose from obtaining agreement to any protocol or regulation by every individual member of IMO, necessitating constant referrals and discussions.

As a further 'for instance', transference of ballast water across the world remains a top priority. It has already been shown that when an oil cargo is discharged then, in order 'to bring the tanker down to her marks' or efficiently cover her bulbous bow and rudder, sea water has to be taken on board from the port where she had discharged into the ballast tanks and pumped out upon arriving at her loading port. This transference has been under investigation for many years, with particular reference to examining effects on the local seas of micro-organisms that have inevitably also been transported across the oceans. An International Ballast Water Management Convention has been in force for some years now, and new designs of supertanker hulls remain under review, examining methods of eliminating the carriage of ballast water in the first place. This has been extended to all classes of ships to test pollution avoidance of the oceans by chemicals, sewage or even litter yet still operate a sustainable ship.

Methods of avoiding atmospheric contamination have led to the exploration into how flue gases may be used not only to improve the 1973–74 introduction of inert gas into cargo tanks, but tests have been made successfully into using this to run the tanker itself. Regulations have been introduced covering the entrance into enclosed tank spaces, so helping to avoid crew members being overcome by dangerous fumes.

Other areas of seafaring continue to become subject to regulation: enhanced computerisation that contributes towards the safety of navigation, ship routing and satellite-based weather forecasting. Other areas totally unforeseen during my seafaring days have been confronted, such as piracy control, voyage data recorders, automatic identification system (AIS) aboard most classes of ships, and more recently maritime cyber risk management, to name but a few.

So the IMO that evolved during my service aboard VLCCs remains far from dead; in fact, this organisation never stands still. It goes from strength to strength and, through necessity, has made all classes of marine tankers subject to the most stringent safety regulations of any industry in the world. I continue to keep in touch with serving deck and engineering officers and am often left pondering that, yes – inevitably – the tanker trades have altered out of much recognition from my days, but the changes have definitely been for the best, benefitting not only those who work across the world's flag states, but additionally the millions worldwide who are served.

GLOSSARY

AB Able-Bodied Seaman. A deck hand with three years' experience possessing an AB Certificate awarded after passing the appropriate test.

Admiralty Pilots Colloquial name for the 72 volumes of Admiralty Sailing Directions covering all navigational areas of the world's surface. They are published by the UK Hydrographic Office and regularly updated, and are intended for use aboard all ships over 150grt amplifying details given on Admiralty charts containing information essential to safe navigation often unavailable in publications elsewhere.

Boat Drills Safety drills where the boats are lowered from their davits to the boat deck and checked so they are available for any emergencies. On deep-sea dry-cargo ships they are scheduled to occur every two weeks, and every week on all tankers.

Cleaner/Wiper A rating employed to help maintain machinery in the engine-room.

Con the ship Navigating the vessel without direct reference to charts, usually in the final stages of close-quarter collision situations or berthing/ anchoring operations

Deck/Navigating Officer A name given to the same officer: on deck when he is supervising cargo/berthing operations, or when navigating the ship in the wheelhouse.

Flag State The country where any ship is registered and subject to its laws.

Foam Monitor/Pipe One of a number of fire extinguishing control monitors served by special pipes issuing either foam or water.

Honkers Colloquialism for the port of Hong Kong.

IMO International Maritime Organisation created originally in 1948 to regulate all aspects of safety at sea, including navigation, crew certification and environmental protection.

Knot A distance of one nautical mile in one hour.

Lascari 1 An Asian seaman equivalent to the rating of AB.

Le Bassurelle Light–Vessel/Float An important weigh-point marking the eight-mile long Bassurelle shoal off the French coast, and used for altering course when leaving the English Channel and entering the Dover Strait.

MARPOL 73/78 Tanker Regulations introduced by IMO in 1973 and amended 1978 governing the safety of the environment from marine pollution.

Monkey Island A part of any deep-sea ship above the wheelhouse housing the magnetic compass.

Nm Nautical mile. A distance at sea measured along one minute of latitude at the Equator of 6080 feet (or 1852m) with sub-divisions of ten units, each comprising the length of one cable.

Nore An area lying east-north-eastwards of the Isle of Grain in the approach channels to the Rivers Thames and Medway. In the northern section midway between Southend and Shoeburyness there lie two deep-water anchorages for VLCCs.

OOW Officer-of-the-Watch – Title of the duty officer in charge of the vessel under the Master's jurisdiction on the bridge at sea, and in port or anchorages.

PGFO A log-book abbreviation indicating the tanker is bound to or from the Persian Gulf For Orders. This means she has sailed without having a designated port, which is normally advised by radio message once the cargo loading or discharging has been finalised.

Secunny An Asian rating equivalent to a Leading Seaman usually assigned to a watch-keeping officer who steers the ship, or acts as lookout or performing general duties.

Smoke Helmet This is worn when entering a compartment or cargo tank where the existence of dangerous fumes might exist. It is usually included in routine drills practiced aboard tankers every week following boat drills.

SOLAS Regulations Issued by IMO governing all issues covering safety of life at sea.

Sounding Pipes These are situated along the length of the main-deck on any dry-cargo ship giving access to below deck tanks helping assess levels of water.

Sparks The ship's radio officer.

Scuppers The lower recesses of the ship where tanks are situated accessed for measuring purposes by sounding pipes.

Stretcher Rescue Another weekly alternative drill in which a human sized/weight dummy is placed in any place aboard ship where crew are likely to work and encounter possible accidents.

Weigh-Point A position on a ship's course-line indicating where a major change of course is required.

ABOUT THE AUTHOR

Ray Solly enjoyed a first career as a navigating officer in the Merchant Navy, serving as chief or second mate aboard deep-sea dry-cargo vessels and coasters. But this book resulted from three out of a number of voyages made as a third and second navigating officer on board Chandris of England's 286,000sdwt VLCC *Rania Chandris* from June 1973, supplemented by experiences on other tankers of equal size. Working aboard ships of this class proved the highlight of his seafaring career. The experiences also provided valuable experience upon which became based a third career as non-fiction marine author of traditionally published books and numerous articles. The twenty years in between were spent as a residential schoolmaster serving two independent schools in Worcester and Kent.

OTHER BOOKS BY RAY SOLLY

Supertankers: Anatomy and Operation (Witherby: 2001).

Picturesque Harbours (Frith: 2002).

Gravesend: A History of Your Town (Frith: 2002).

Mariner's Launch (Whittles: 2005).

BP Shipping: A Group Fleet History (co-author) (Chatham: 2005).

Mariner's Voyage (Whittles: 2008).

Athel Line: A Fleet History (History: 2009).

Nothing over the Side: Examining Safe Crude Oil Tankers (Whittles: 2010).

Manual of Tanker Operations (co-author) (Brown, Son, Ferguson: 2011).

Mariner's Rest (Whittles: 2012).

BP's Early Large Tankers: Ships and Life Aboard (Ships Illustrated: 2015).

Questing for the Dove: A Spiritual Journey (Lighthouse Christian: 2018).

COMING SOON

Crude Oil Tankers: A Pictorial Miscellany (World/Ships) (12/2019).

BP Shipping: The Golden Years 1945–1975 (Whittles) (2020).

Tate and Lyle's Secret Navy: The Athel Line (World Ships) (2021).

Living the River Thames (in planning stage).

www.raysollyseabooks.com

You may also enjoy …

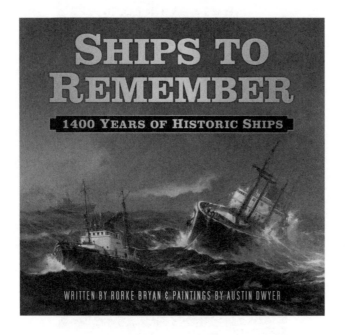

978 0 7509 6590 3

Spanning 1,400 years, *Ships to Remember* includes historic ships and events such as the catastrophic sinking and eventual recovery of the *Vasa*, Nelson's triumph at the Battle of Copenhagen, Darwin's epochal voyage on HMS *Beagle* and the pivotal Second World War relief of Malta by the tanker *Ohio*.

You may also enjoy …

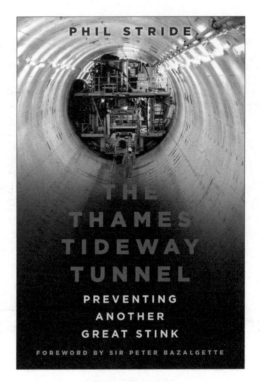

PHIL STRIDE

THE
THAMES
TIDEWAY
TUNNEL

PREVENTING
ANOTHER
GREAT STINK

FOREWORD BY SIR PETER BAZALGETTE

978 0 7509 8981 7

The inside story on the Thames Tideway Tunnel from the very start to breaking ground, and all the steps along the way. Written by a leading civil engineer, this is a unique chance both to see behind the scenes of an civil engineering project that will transform the environment, and to meet the people who've taken the project forward over the last ten years.